DATES
Ag 6 LISTS What's the
Y JOKES
STORY
ACES 281-
ncoded PHONE #
24 SHORT RETRIEVED 113
TERM
mes Places LONG TERM
SOUNDS ADDRESS
TIME GOaV
POEMS
NUMBERS LETTERS
km W q MUSIC
I'M LOST RECALL U S
AGAIN FIRST
B KISS
8x9=
Q $ Z HOW DO I?
36 TEACHERS
OLD MOVIE STAR
SCRIPTURES W T p h
LOOP
ICENSE # # q 12
M A
WHERE I WHERE WE MET
PARKED
THE CAR RECOLLECTION

LISTS
JOKES
What's t
COMBINATI
HISTORY
FACES
281-
PHONE #
Encoded
24
SHORT TERM
RETRIEVED
Names
Places
LONG TER
SOUNDS
TIME
POEMS
ADDRES
NUMBERS
LETTE
MUSIC
I'M LOST AGAIN
RECALL
FIRST KISS
8 x 9 =
36
HOW DO I?
TEACHERS
OLD MOVIE STAR
SCRIPTURES
LOOP
LICENSE#
WHERE I PARKED THE CAR
WHERE WE M
RECOLLECTIO

# MEMORY!

A HANDBOOK FOR SENIORS

A SUPER SENIOR

# MEMORY!

Become a Senior Memory Whiz
in minutes a day!

Short chapters, easy-to-learn techniques.

JOHN LESLIE

A Super Senior Memory!
Copyright © 2017 by John Leslie
All rights reserved. No part of this book may be reproduced or transmitted in any form or by any means without written permission of the author.
Cover and book design by Ron Folsom

ISBN 978-0-692-87974-0

## Foreword

This is not a book filled with magical ways to remember everything.

It is a book filled with **Here's how** techniques that a willing senior can use to make life's later years filled with memories that are not a wisp of smoke from the past, but real memories filled with the details of life.

Seniors can, with just a little effort, finish life alert, able to recall names, faces, events–all those memories that make life worth living.

There are some memory aids that lend themselves to non-technical solutions. Think of a pencil and paper. That's a great way and doesn't require learning anything you haven't known since you were in school.

The iPhone has solved a great many memory issues: you can easily record notes, find names, addresses, and phone numbers, and with just a little more effort, record personal data about all your friends. You can depend on your phone to remind you of birthdays, anniversaries, and stuff like that.

Take advantage of every easily-learned, but highly sophisticated technique that's out there.

But you still have to remember names and faces, the outline of your speech, the book you just read or the movie you saw last week. Oh, and there's the car; where did you park it? (But I forgot: you can dictate to your phone recorder where you parked, so, maybe for some of us, that little problem has been solved.)

You can remember the other stuff. You've got a great memory.

***I'll prove it.***

## About the Author

John Leslie continues to explore the role of seniors as they respond to contemporary moral issues. This book, the second in his series on memory, addresses the major concern of most seniors: to be mentally alert as long as they live. Seniors want to live a life that's rich and full. They want to positively participate in a mature quest to remember yesterday's and today's happenings. They want to contribute to life.

This book is written in light, conversational English, just one friend talking to another. The techniques and methods suggestions are made in easy-to-follow steps.

It is his belief that aging citizens are the cornerstone of the future as they become a dominant force in American politics. But they must earn the right to leadership by expressing their views on contemporary issues. A mind that remembers is an important part of evaluating and understanding the past and developing intelligent responses to the future.

John and his wife, Janice, reside in Houston, Texas. Their three sons are also Texans.

# Table of Contents

Foreword .................................................................................. i
About the Author ................................................................... iii

| Chapter | **Section One** | |
|---|---|---|
| | Preface .................................................................. ix | |
| 1 | What Are You Looking For? ................................ 1 | |
| 2 | Minutes a Day to a Better Memory ..................... 3 | |
| 3 | The Easy First Step to a Better Memory ............ 4 | |
| 4 | Start with a Dose of Reality ................................. 5 | |
| 5 | A Great Idea to Help You Get Started ............... 6 | |
| 6 | Important Information for Your Journey .......... 8 | |
| 7 | Intelligence and Wisdom .................................. 10 | |
| 8 | How Smart Are You? Are You a Genius or Just Smart? .. 13 | |
| 9 | Getting Ready ..................................................... 15 | |
| 10 | Your Great Memory ........................................... 16 | |
| 11 | You Can't Learn Unless You Can Remember What You Learned ............................................. 17 | |
| 12 | What is Memory? ............................................... 18 | |
| 13 | The Memory Process ......................................... 21 | |
| 14 | What Do You Want to be Able to Do After You've Finished this Memory Book? ............ 22 | |
| 15 | Why? What Is Your Motivation? ...................... 23 | |
| 16 | Learner Types Part 1 .......................................... 28 | |
| 17 | Learner Types Part 2 .......................................... 29 | |
| 18 | Jump on The Bandwagon .................................. 31 | |
| 19 | Why Do We Forget? — Part 1 ........................... 33 | |

| 20 | Why Do We Forget?—Part 2 | 36 |
| --- | --- | --- |
| 21 | Why Do We Forget?—Part 3 | 39 |
| 22 | Take A Nap. It Will Improve Your Memory | 41 |
| 23 | The Five Stages of Sleep | 43 |
| 24 | Evaluating Memory | 45 |

**Section Two**

| 25 | What's Next? | 47 |
| --- | --- | --- |
| 26 | The Two-Step Process to Make a Memory | 48 |
| 27 | Using Your Memory | 49 |
| 28 | Memory Vocabulary | 50 |
| 29 | Memory Mnemonics | 58 |
| 30 | More on Mnemonics | 62 |
| 31 | Reverse Acronyms | 67 |
| 32 | Chunking | 69 |
| 33 | Repeating as a Way to Remember | 72 |
| 34 | Link, Memory Palace, or Peg Word? | 74 |
| 35 | Link Method and the Story Memory Methods | 75 |
| 36 | Memory Palace | 78 |
| 37 | The Consonant and Number Peg System | 83 |
| 38 | How the Peg Word System Works | 85 |
| 39 | Your Own Proof of the Pudding | 90 |
| 40 | Remember Numbers, Long or Short Ones | 91 |
| 41 | More on Numbers | 94 |
| 42 | Keyword | 96 |
| 43 | Some Other Ways to Remember | 102 |
| 44 | Forgetting the Routine Stuff is Easy, But Don't | 104 |
| 45 | Remember the Contents of a Book | 106 |

| | | |
|---|---|---|
| 46 | Recall Word for Word | 109 |
| 47 | Remember Names and Faces | 113 |
| 48 | Words, Where Did They Go? | 119 |
| 49 | Forgetting to Carry Out the Humdrum Tasks | 121 |
| 50 | A 30-Second Memory Techniques Summary | 122 |
| 51 | Helpful Conclusions | 125 |
| 52 | Miscellaneous Conclusion<br>The World Memory Championship Criteria | 127 |

## Preface

I can't stress too much: ***all learning is based on memory.*** It's true; you can take it to the bank! Just put information into your head in a way you can get it out. I'm glad you're reading this book because you're going to learn how to do just that!

As a senior, most of us really appreciate learning in small increments. As you'll discover, this book does just that. We work at learning something new for a while and then take a break. After a bit, we restart the learning process. I suggest you do this several times a day. Seniors can pace themselves in a way that seems about right for their age. But it's also scientific. Short learning periods are good. We want to learn. And we will, using the Kaizen process, updated for seniors.

Learning in small bites is easy. Do that using the memory techniques you'll be learning and you'll be a memory whiz in no time at all.

If you can, set aside a learning period where you can give your complete attention to the chapters of the book. Avoid interruptions. It's the best way to develop new pathways to your mind.

I suspect the reason you're reading this book is to be able to share the worth of your life with family and friends. As a senior, you've learned many of life's lessons the hard way: you experienced them. Being able to confidently speak knowledgeably about what you know and remember about life is worthwhile. But there's more than just recalling the past. You want to demonstrate that your life experiences the happenings of your past analyzed and evaluated by current events have value for the present. As a senior, it is important to speak confidentially about what you know about life and how your knowledge fits into a world that is changing rapidly. You have a contribution to make ... today. Your knowledge can help loved ones and friends make necessary social and intellectual transitions in real time. And you won't be repeating the same story over and over; you'll remember past and current events and do the mental analysis that makes you a charming conversationalist.

You are a leader who walks on fire. You will be a sage!

At the end of each chapter there is a text box filled with information that probably does not relate to the chapter contents.

It's meant to create a break in your learning experience. These are not memory tips or techniques; they are vignettes from life. Take them; use them if they help.

When you can, visualize new information. Things that have action and color go easier into your mind. This is a scientific fact.

Work on a memory issue with the appropriate memory tools you'll learn. There are lots of memory methods and all are not included in this book. From the techniques used by professionals, I have selected the ones I think are of most benefit to seniors.

And like everything, frequent use insures recall. The rule: learn it, use it, practice, practice, practice.

Improving memory is not an overwhelming task. It's easy; your mind is actively waiting for you to present it with new things. When you learn or do something new, your identity changes; it shifts to a new knowledge level. This change is known as "cognitive dissonance." When we change our actions, our minds change to match the actions.

Virtual memory puts information in lot of places in your head. Your challenge is where did it put the information so you can get it back? It's easier to remember things you can visualize and associate with other memories. And there are ways to convert the intangibles into visible action. Do it by substitution, creating something out of proportion, by exaggeration, with accelerated movement, etc. You know how. These are the things you've been doing all your life.

You were born with intelligence. Some of us are born with more intelligence than others. There are objective ways to measure intelligence, like IQ tests. And there are many ways to expand your intelligence, regardless of age. Really.

Being good at more at than one thing is an indication of creative breath and is an identifier of mental status. The test of "smartness" is how intelligence is used, usually displayed as creativeness. Creativity separates genius from intelligent.

Put information into your mind. Get it out when you need it. That's what everyone wants to do. We want a rational and emotionally adaptive mindset that enables us to objectively (accurately) recall what's in our head. You're beginning the journey that will make you proud of your mind!

# Chapter 1
## WHAT ARE YOU LOOKING FOR?

**Virtually all learning is based on memory.**
**All memory is based on visualization and association.**
**Any new information can be remembered if it is visually associated to something already known.**
**A trained memory knows how to do just that!**

*That's you ....*

I hope you're not reading this book of memory self-improvement techniques because you're afraid. What do you want from your memory?

Whatever your reason, I'm glad you're here. Together we will get rid of any self-doubts you may have about remembering. Unless medical issues intervene, by the time you get to the last page of this book, you will know how to remember anything. "How to" is the key. Putting the how-to techniques to work is squarely on your shoulders.

Scientists agree your mind can be in only one of three states: unconscious, aware, or self-aware. Self-awareness is what we're looking for. (Don't worry about the other two stages.) When you become self-aware, you are unique. "How to" be self-aware gets a priority. Start by asking the questions that make consciousness expand. When that happens, the possibilities are infinite. You don't know what the questions are? You will.

Do you remember your first boy/girl kiss? I'm not talking about the name of that lucky person, or where it happened. I'm referring to the emotion that makes a memory stick in your mind. (I'll bet you do remember that first kiss. But what was the price of unleaded gas that day?) There's a lot more to come on the subject of creating the emotion that enables you to remember.

As you go through each chapter, shoot for intentionally becoming "detached" from today's reality for a while. Detachment gives you the opportunity to step back from your emotions and create new pathways in your mind. When you're there creating new memories, it's special. It's a higher level of experience, and a place where all of life is meaningful.

Detached, you're on a first name basis with many emotions. Better than that, you can control your emotions. You'll understand fear, anger, happiness, curiosity, and the spiritual feelings of bliss, compassion, and wonder. Those experiences are special, believe me.

Later, question yourself about how you felt at that "detached" time. That's reality making.

Reality making has no upper limit. If you think of reality as a limitation, it's a limitation you create. Your mind continues to evolve and develop. There are no limitations.

> Living with other people presents difficulties for most of us. Families can be unrelentingly hard, and many people relish being single and free. But at some point, we see that this freedom isn't what it appears to be, and decide to marry, or we simply fall in love.
>
> At the beginning, we are so courteous with each other, but over time, familiarity diminishes the niceties, then we start to annoy each other with careless words and actions. In many cases, familiarity indeed breeds contempt.
>
> To avoid this disaster, why don't you begin and end each day together? If it's not possible to spend much of every day together, you can make sure you share the same room at night. That way, whatever you think of your day, it will always be contextualized by your relationship, giving your life structure and support.

## Chapter 2
### Minutes A Day To A Better Memory

I'll bet one of your secret thoughts is that you wish your memory were better. You're tired of forgetting names, appointments, or small details like where you left your car in the shopping center parking lot. And it would be nice to remember the plot of a book or movie a few days later.

You've read about memory methods or pills that will take "care" of your problem and correctly discounted them. And you don't want to commit to a difficult program that involves memorizing many things to make your memory better. In fact, you're not sure you could. That's a problem, too!

**There's another way. An easy way.** This book uses a neat learning methodology that's been around since the "40's." It's the technique developed by Dr. William Deming that was used to speed up U.S. manufacturing in World War II and subsequently exported to Japan. It's responsible for Japan's resurgence as an extremely cost-effective provider. The Japanese call it "Kaizen." It is a proven way to improve anything ... **a small step at a time.** Kaizen represents change in tiny, comfortable, and painless increments.

This book uses the Kaizen methodology: **spend a few minutes every day improving your memory and I guarantee your memory will get better effortlessly.**

*An easy-to-read book about Kaizen is "One Small Step Can Change Your Life: The Kaizen Way" by Robert Maurer. It was published in 2004 by Workman Publishing Company,*

---

Prayer is not a "spare wheel" that you pull out when in trouble, but a "steering wheel" that directs us to the right path throughout the journey. Live simply. Love generously. Care deeply. Speak kindly. Leave the rest to God. When GOD solves your problems, you have faith in HIS abilities; when GOD doesn't solve your problems, HE has faith in your abilities.

# Chapter 3
## THE EASY FIRST STEP TO A BETTER MEMORY

As a senior citizen, you probably don't learn things now as easily as you did 20 years ago, However, on the plus side, you didn't get where you are today without learning a thing or two. People expect you to be a source of "old" information; they don't expect you to be actively working to increase your knowledge of current issues.

**But they don't know you. They don't know the inquisitive mind you have; they don't know of your interest in everything, and that you know a lot about many relevant topics.**

Even at your age, you still have substantial knowledge and are quite interested in expanding your topical memory.

This series will help. **Here's how:**

> You'll learn how to remember things that can be **visualized,** and
> 
> How to increase your understanding of topics that represent general and specific knowledge (as opposed to philosophic situations and issues not easily quantified).

The first topic is easier; we'll start with it.

Congratulate yourself for your decision to continue learning. Pat yourself on the back. That's all you have to do today.

---

**Family** isn't always blood relations. Family can be the people in your life who want you in theirs. Family are the ones who accept you for who you are. They're the ones who would do anything to see you smile and who love you no matter what.

Be thankful for what you have. Don't wait until it's too late to tell someone how much you love them and how much you care about them, because when you or they are gone, no matter how much we shout and cry, they won't hear you anymore.

## Chapter 4
### START WITH A DOSE OF REALITY

In very non-technical terms, think of memory like this: Memory is your way to easily personalize things that reflect your understanding. That means your understanding of lists, dates, choices, rules, faces, or voices ... stuff like that.

There are ways to recover from memory the plot of a novel, or to conceptualize using two or three different theories, or to ponder about the creation of the universe, or anything. In all likelihood, there is a memory technique that is "just right" for any situation you'll encounter.

You'll learn the methodology for each memory category, but the "things" tools the way to create and remember will be the most valuable to you, and, luckily, easily learned.

To become proficient in your favorite memory aids, you need to practice every day. In fact, to become proficient, you need to practice two or three times per day. The sessions don't have to be long, five minutes or so will do. Spread out the sessions ... morning, noon, and night. The secret: practice, practice, practice!

What you can expect as a result: easy familiarity in a week, relative competency in two weeks, proficiency in a month!

Using what you'll learn as you go through this book, you'll **easily** personalize systems that reflect your memory of events or data. You'll also learn ways to **recover from your memory** the stuff you've stored away.

Your memory will be your partner as you develop new and exciting learning techniques. You'll have unique skills....

---

Don't be bothered too much by others' mistakes. It is certainly hard in the heat of the moment to turn the other cheek. But, for the sake of your own health and happiness, forgive and forget as soon as you can. Otherwise, you will only be increasing your blood pressure.

# Chapter 5
## A GREAT IDEA TO GET YOU STARTED

Sometimes the idea of doing something new can feel so overwhelming that you wind up choosing not to do anything. Changing mental habits certainly fits the overwhelming part. Here's a great idea: **commit to doing just a tiny new thing each day,** like read at least one chapter of this book. Move a small step forward at your own pace with one of the techniques (remember "Kaizen," the proven way to improve anything ... **a small step at a time**). Absorb new memory information in tiny, comfortable, and painless increments.

Here's something else you'll quickly discover: memory improvement is not as overwhelming as you'd thought. As you learn new things, you're participating in what is called "identity shifting." When you start doing new, disciplined, life-improving actions, your mind begins to shift and you see yourself as a disciplined, life-improving person. Your subconscious says, "The old me did not have this discipline. But wow! this new me does!"

There's a famous psychological theory called "cognitive dissonance," which explains this identity shift. It goes like this: "We humans don t like to have a disparity between our thoughts and our actions, so when we change our actions, we change our thoughts to match them."

For example: If Human A starts to do a loving something for Human B, Human A (according to the cognitive dissonance theory), starts saying to itself, "Geez, I must surely like Human B if I'm now doing a loving something for them!" As a result, according to the theory, Human A will wind up liking Human B a wee bit more.

Likewise, if you convince yourself to do positive, disciplined actions, then your brain—via the perks of cognitive dissonance—will start to tell you, "Geez, I must be a positive, disciplined person if I'm doing positive, disciplined actions." Eventually you will wind up being a wee bit more positive and disciplined! And you'll like yourself even more!

The memory techniques described in this series were created for easy learning. To help, you'll notice there is some repetition from chapter to chapter. This is not accidental.

*As you go along, you'll absorb methodologies for creating a happier, more successful, more memorable life with total ease. Sprinkled within the pages are ideas from Aristotle, Martin Seligman, Viktor Frankl, Bertrand Russel, Jung, Freud, biology, Buddhism, cognitive therapy, Jesus Christ, Darwinism, Neuro Linguistic Programming, neuroscience, positive psychology, sociology, quantum physics, western philosophy, Zen of Bazooka Joe – and the best ideas from some of the world's memory experts!*

**Don't you feel happier already? Sure you do.**

---

Seventy-eight years and 724 participants later, a Harvard study reached some conclusions about what makes us happy. It's this: **good relationships are the key to leading happier, healthier, and more fulfilling lives.**

Social connections are really good for us. Loneliness can have the opposite effect. People who are more socially connected to family, friends, and community are happier, physically healthier, and live longer than people who are less well connected.

In relationships, it's quality over quantity. It's not just the number of friends you have or whether or not you're in a committed relationship, it's the quality of your close relationships that matters.

Good relationships are good for the body and mind. The memories of people in good relationships stay sharper for longer.

## Chapter 6
### IMPORTANT INFORMATION FOR YOUR JOURNEY

You'll read this a hundred times: "Virtually all learning is based on memory. All memory is based on the visualization and association of one thing to another." It's true.

Creating a memory event connects two things, a name to a face, a phone number or an address to a person or company, your reaction to an event, or the definition or meaning to a word. The basic rule of memory is that **you can remember any new piece of information if it is associated in some outlandish way to something you already know or remember.**

Easy-to-learn memory techniques will enable you to create images and consciously associate the image of what you want to remember to an image of something you already know. Once the techniques are habits, you'll have a trained memory, and all learning will be easier for you the rest of your life.

It is easy to remember things that are physical or have significant meaning and can be pictured. It is not easy to remember or picture intangible things. However, there are ways to **substitute** tangible images for any intangible thing. *Here's how:*

- Substitute (picture **one item instead of the other; this is a prime rule).**
- Make the image out of proportion (imagine the item as **larger than life).**
- Exaggerate (**millions** instead of one).
- Action (make your item **move**).

Our minds capture information (call it becoming originally aware, a Harry Lorayne concept) and store it in our minds. Nothing you are originally aware of can be forgotten. However, unless there is a way to recall the information, the stored information is worthless.

To whet your interest, let's casually explore some of the techniques you'll be exposed to in detail in the second half of this book. This is an easy introduction.

**Linking** is one way a remembered thought is connected to another thought **in sequence**. This linking technique manifests itself in almost every memory method you'll be learning. The **Memory Palace** is a great example of linking.

**Pegging** is a way thoughts are tied to a tangible image of a number and thus able to be recalled at specific points. Peg words are based on the phonetic alphabet. Numbers are given representative consonant-only sounds (for example, "t" for "1"). The representation will never change and can be used in lots of ways. Pegging is easy-to-learn and is probably the best system for seniors.

**Keywords** take the place of abstract or intangible words or phrases. Keywords involve replacing the intangible with something tangible that substitutes for, sounds like, or reminds you of the abstract or intangible material. The replacement can always be pictured in the mind.

Remember **Names and Faces** by depending on the face to tell you the name. Create a mental picture for names that have meaning. Some names don't have a meaning but remind you of something tangible. For names that have no meaning, create a substitute that can be pictured in your mind. It's not necessary to substitute all the exact name sounds, just the main sounds or elements.

There are other techniques. This book concentrates on the ones most helpful to seniors.

---

Malcomb Gladwell writes, "The success of any kind of social epidemic is heavily dependent on the involvement of people with a particular and rare set of social gifts." He calls these people, "The Law of the Few." Economists call this involvement the "80/20 Principle," which is the idea that in any situation, roughly 80 percent of the "work" will be done by 20 percent of the participants

## Chapter 7
### INTELLIGENCE AND WISDOM

Intelligence is something, some say, we are born with.

On the other hand, at your age, you've acquired **wisdom**, which is far more useful than intelligence. Wisdom is definitely something you've sought to accumulate over a lifetime.

The Berlin Wisdom Project of the late '80s defined wisdom as:

- Spiritual knowledge
- Factual knowledge
- Excellent judgment
- Excellent problem-solving skills
- Ability to learn from experience
- Humility, emotional strength, or the ability to recover from defeat
- Openness and maturity, allowing another to see you as you really are
- A deeper understanding of human nature, including empathy for others and other cultures

However, if you don't think you embody all these qualities, here are six other ways to become wiser:

### 1. Being Social

Research has shown that people who keep more contact with other people display higher levels of wisdom than those who remain more secluded. This may be due to new people constantly giving us new ideas to think about, new information, and new experiences. This exposure enriches the mind and gives us more wisdom.

So, make an effort, if not for others, then for yourself. Stay in touch with old friends, take a course, and stay in contact with those around you. It's the wise thing to do.

### 2. Open mindedness

We're lucky to understand all aspects of a problem without surrendering to personal feelings. An open mind displays true empathy and recognizes everyone has a life story that affects them in some way.

It is not our place to judge. For instance, write down the issues you confront every day. At day's end, take a look at your list with the intent to get a new perspective on each problem. You'll be surprised at what comes to mind. (Doing this every day is not realistic for most of us; try doing it occasionally. The result will be the same. You'll be surprised.)

### 3. "I could be mistaken"

A smart person understands that it is impossible to know everything, and that life always throws you a curve when you least expect it. Acknowledging your mistakes may lead to greater wisdom. Remember, your ability to be wrong shouldn't damage your reputation as a wise person, but should increase it **because** wise people know how to take responsibility for their mistakes. Acknowledge the limits of your knowledge and admit when you are wrong.

### 4. Experiencing new things

While we each have our own personal tastes in books, music, art, or movies, getting familiar with unknown things will broaden our horizons and introduce new world views, new ideas, and new outlooks on life. Whatever it is you almost never read, give it a try. Now is the time to add some real-life experience to things you haven't touched on. Try something new, learn a new skill. It won't just make you wiser, it'll also keep you young!

### 5. Self-awareness

You may say you've had a rich life experience, but when was the last time you really stopped to think of all you've learned throughout life? What are your three biggest failures and your three biggest successes? Without pride or regret, did you use each experience to drive yourself forward? After all, knowing yourself is your biggest challenge.

**6. Know what goes on around you**

The news is often dramatic, misrepresented or depressing. But it's hard to make balanced decisions for yourself and others if you don't learn from your mistakes and of the mistakes of others or of your city, country, and world. Keep updated, read a newspaper, watch the news, or just read a news site online from time to time. Read the articles, not just headlines, and understand how you fit into this bigger world. This awareness is crucial for true wisdom.

**Here's your "to do" list from this chapter:**

Meet someone new (be social).

Discuss your political beliefs with someone (good luck!).

In a discussion, say aloud, "You know, I could be mistaken. You make a great point."

Do something you've never done before.

Review your list of failures and successes. Tell someone about your experiences.

Listen to news from a Republican and a Democratic station. Is there a difference?

Go out for dinner tonight to a place you've never gone before. You'll never forget it.

What does all this have to do with memory? Go figure....

---

Everything has a reason, a purpose. Take life as it comes. Accept yourself as you are, and accept others for what they are. You know that one day you'll have to leave this world. Many of us are afraid of death. Don't be. We worry that our spouse and children will be unable to withstand their loss. But the truth is that though they may painfully mourn for some time, time heals everything and they will carry on. Remember, no one leaves this world alive

## Chapter 8

### HOW SMART ARE YOU?

### ARE YOU A GENIUS OR JUST SMART?

You're intelligent. But are you a genius? What are the signs of genius? Are you a genius, or just really, really smart? Is memory an indicator?

Most highly creative people are **polymaths**—they enjoy and excel at a range of challenging activities. (A polymath is a person whose expertise spans a significant number of different subject areas. Such a person is known to draw on complex bodies of knowledge to solve specific problems.)

In a survey of scientists at all levels of achievement, only about one-sixth engage in a secondary activity of an artistic or creative nature. In contrast, nearly all Nobel Prize winners in science have at least one other creative activity they pursue seriously. They paint or write non-scientific prose...stuff like that.

Creative breadth is an important but understudied component of genius. It's a requirement for genius status.

Mention **"intelligence,"** and the average person assumes you are speaking of that top one or two percent, those whose IQ score is over 145. However, most intelligence researchers do their research with those whose average IQ score is around 100. They focus their attention on the lower to middle portion of the distribution. (That's most of us!)

Why? One reason is because of the correlations between individual abilities measured on IQ tests. The actual overall ability levels of the persons taking the test are the strongest among those whose IQ scores are 110 and below.

Scientists looked at the attributes of successful, intelligent, creative people and figured out that they had something going for them that other highly intelligent people did not. They made this trait the difference between "intelligent" and "genius."

What, then, is the definition of "intelligence?" Is it:
An IQ score?
Computational ability?
Being able to talk your way out of a speeding ticket?
Knowing how to handle a crisis effectively?
Arguing a convincing case before a jury?

Maybe the answer is all the above. Dr Robert Sternberg believes that **intelligence is comprised of three facets**, which he called the Tribrachic Theory of Intelligence:

1. *Analytical Ability* (the results from IQ tests).

2. *Creativity.*

3. *Practical Ability* (being able to use analytical skills and creativity to effectively solve novel problems).

In a nutshell, just **intelligence** (as most people measure it today) is not enough to set a person apart and raise them to the level of genius.

Someone could have an IQ of 170, yet get lost inside a paper bag, or not have the ability to hold a conversation with anyone other than a dog. It was Albert Einstein's creativity that placed him far ahead of his intelligent scientist peers.

**Creativity is the defining feature that separates mere intelligence from utter genius.**

I'll bet you are very creative.

(I wrote about "intelligence" and "genius" in Chapter 7 of my first book on memory, "Aging Memory." One conclusion from that chapter was, "There are lots of us worrying about our aging memories, and more are joining the worriers every year. By 2050, 40% of 65-year-olds are likely to reach age 90.")

---

How will you start the next day fully in love if you can't end the day right? Think why you love your partner before you go to bed. Tell them you love them, and make contact -- a kiss, a hug -- or whatever works for you.

## Chapter 9
### GETTING READY!

Let's Get Down and Dirty ...

Let's talk about memory.

**You'll want to read everything from here on. By the time you've finished this book, you'll know more than you ever thought you would about memory.**

That's good.

You'll be glad you read every word.

Really.

*You're getting new information according to the Kaizen methodology... a little at a time.*

*Understanding memory isn't easy, and it'll take some time. But, at the end, you'll have a layman's understanding of this complex part of your body. The really good part is you're on a path to learn the best ways to put information into your memory and, more importantly, how to get it out!*

---

As we grow older and wiser, we realize that wearing a $300 or a $30.00 watch ... they both tell the same time. Whether we carry a $300 or $30.00 wallet/handbag, the amount of money inside is the same. Whether we drink a bottle of $300 or $10 wine, the hangover is the same. Whether the house we live in is 300 or 3,000 sq. ft., loneliness is the same.

True inner happiness does not come from the material things of this world. It's when you have family, buddies, old friends, brothers, sisters, and cousins who you chat with, laugh with, talk with, cry with, sing songs with, talk about north, south, east, west, or heaven and earth ... that is true happiness!

# Chapter 10

## YOUR GREAT MEMORY!

If you have negative thoughts about your memory, you need to get rid of them. *Here's how:*

*Develop a relational and emotionally adaptive mindset.* That'll do it.

(Those words may not mean anything to you ... now. They will. And when they do, you'll be convinced **you have a great memory!**)

Maybe you said to yourself, **"What's a relational and emotionally adaptive mindset?"** Whatever it is, at my age, how do I develop that?"

*Stay tuned.*

Others have successfully used the techniques you'll be learning and now **easily** remember lots of stuff! When you finish this book, you'll have a confident self-image and be considered a sage among your families and friends!

*That's you, isn't it? You are a sage!*

---

Here's a prayer for today: "Father, Thank you for each and every day. You have blessed us here on earth. Thank you for your tender mercies. Thank you for giving us friends and family to share joys and sorrows with. I ask you to bless my friends, relatives, brothers and sisters in Christ and those I care deeply for.

"Where there is joy, give them continued joy. Where there is pain or sorrow, give them your peace and mercy. Where there is self-doubt, release in them renewed confidence. Where there is need, fulfill their needs. Bless their homes, families, finances, their goings and their comings.

"In Jesus' name, Amen."

## Chapter 11
### YOU CAN'T LEARN UNLESS YOU CAN REMEMBER WHAT YOU LEARNED

Virtually **all** learning is based on memory. (You've heard this before?)

**All memory is based on visualization and association.** Any new piece of information can be remembered if it is visually and vividly associated to something already known. Remember this.

Learning how to associate new information to known information is the key to a trained memory. You're going to get the key.

The **value of memory** is judged in one of two ways: either subjectively or objectively. You'll read this again and again:

> **Subjective memory** is our perception of how well we do. Subjective memory is **not** measurable. Bragging is an example of using subjective memory. Shoot for objective memory.

> **Objective memory** is a measurable indicator of performance. In an objective evaluation, there is a "score."

**New information can best be remembered by consciously associating it with something already known or remembered. If remembered, information can be measured for accuracy. It is "objective memory."**

---

Do regular acts of kindness. Spending money on others makes us happier than spending money on ourselves. Doing small acts of kindness increases life satisfaction. Hold the door for the person behind you, say thank you and mean it when you get your drink from the coffee shop: Pick up your colleague's favorite snack and leave it on their desk for them. Even the smallest nice gesture can make someone's day.

## Chapter 12
### What Is Memory?

Answering the question, "What is memory?" is hard and involves explaining a lot of things. This chapter starts the ball rolling, and the explanations will continue for a while. The explanations won't be technical, but what you'll be reading is not the most exciting prose you've ever read. But let's get going.

Remembering anything starts when you:

**Encode it.** This means taking the event (whatever it is) into your head (you use your senses to do this), mentally organizing it, and, finally, intentionally storing it away somewhere in your memory (not necessarily in one place).

**Recall it.** Once you've encoded your new memory into your head, you need to be able to **recall it. Recall** means bringing the event back from memory later.

You'll be getting lots of advice on encoding, storing, and recall. Lots.

Think of it this way: **memory is your personal representation of everything stored in your head and the way you dig it up for use at a later time.**

Encode it. Store it. Recall it. Easy to say, but some of us need help doing it. And help is on the way. As you may have noticed, some explanations are frequently repeated. There's a reason for it: you need to understand so you can use this understanding to your advantage. Repetition helps.

Memory is a process governed by multiple systems in your brain. It's so complex; the intricacies of memory are not completely understood (but progress continues). With a contemporary under-standing of how memory works, you're in a good position to benefit and participate in the techniques that will do the most for you, some of them centuries old, others hot off the press.

**Here goes....**

Memory is a process of storage and retrieval of information and experience. Information makes its way into your memory through your senses. It is then processed by multiple systems in your brain and stored for later use.

Memory is stored (encoded; remember the definition?) according to themes, such as:

**Time** (when something happened),

**Category** (animal, plant, mineral), or

**Function** (a hammer is used to pound nails).

The different memory storage themes represent complex individual memory systems within the brain **that you control.**

Retrieving information encoded within one or more of these themes is dependent upon knowing the file that was **consciously** chosen to hold newly learned information. That's your challenge: intentionality.

In other words, you can choose **where** in your mind a particular memory is stored. It can be in a folder that already exists, or you can create a new one. This choice is a very important part of the memory process. Think of it as **associating** new information to already-in-place information or placing new information in a new location you intentionally created **in order to make retrieval easier.**

If you don't make this intentional choice, the system does it for you. All the information in your head is stored **somewhere.** If you don't know where it is, finding it again is difficult, but not impossible. Sometimes, it may seem to be.

You need a way to get a stored memory back. The ease and accuracy of retrieval depend upon your effectiveness at the initial encoding and your **conscious** choice of a retrieval method. That's the challenge we'll be working on.

In review: to remember anything, there are two essential steps:

First, **encode** whatever it is you want to remember.

Second, once encoded, **recall** it.

One more time:

> **Encoding** involves taking the information in (you use your senses to do this), organizing it, and, finally, storing it away somewhere you'll remember.

> **Recall** means getting the information back at a later time (this is the real problem; it's stored somewhere, but where?).

**Memory is your personal representation of everything outside yourself and your unique way to dig it up for use later.**

Encode it. Recall it. Easy to say, but some of us need help with both topics. There are lots of ways to put stuff into your head. You need to find the way (or ways) best for you. Coming up is the first look at your options.

Memory is a very complicated subject being investigated by many bright people. The memory we're talking about represents what *you* want to recall on *your* terms. Don't sweat the technical details and don't concern yourself with myths. However, if you want to explore the subject further, I have written about the "myths" of memory in my book, "Aging Memory." Also, see Kenneth Higble's book, "Your Memory; How It Works & How to Improve It."

---

Often, satisfaction with life is tied to your frame of reference and the comparisons you make. If you're trying to "keep up with the Joneses," and the Joneses are millionaires, it's very difficult to stay happy and satisfied with your place in life. It's not so hard if you're volunteering your time to help those in need. By that comparison, you have so much.

One quick and simple way to turn your mood around is to change your expectations and comparisons. Instead of looking at what you don't have, Look at all you **do** have. There will always be people who have more than you in one area of life or another, but many have less. Celebrate the benefits of gratitude and change the way you view what you have (and don't have). You'll experience more happiness right away.

# Chapter 13
## THE MEMORY PROCESS

How are you doing with that "little bit at a time" thing? You know, the Kaizen Method.

You've noticed by now that some points are repeated from time to time (like this little notice itself that has already been repeated a time or two). It's not by accident.

***I hope the process is working for you.***

---

Albert Einstein said this: "The most beautiful thing we can experience is the mysterious. It is the source of all true art and all science. He to whom this emotion is a stranger, who can no longer pause to wonder and stand rapt in awe, is as good as dead; his eyes are closed.

"A man's ethical behavior should be based effectually on sympathy, education, and social ties; no religious basis is necessary. Man would indeed be in a poor way if he had to be restrained by fear of punishment and hope of reward after death.

"The further the spiritual evolution of mankind advances, the more certain it seems to me that the path to genuine religiosity does not lie through the fear of life, the fear of death, and blind faith, but through striving after rational knowledge."

## Chapter 14

### WHAT DO YOU WANT TO BE ABLE TO DO AFTER YOU'VE FINISHED THIS MEMORY BOOK?

Another short lesson.

What new or improved memory skill do you want to have by the time you've finished reading this book?

Think about it. Try to be profound, not frivolous.

I've asked you this question to get you thinking **again** about why you want to improve your memory. Writing it down will prove to be both intrinsic and extrinsic motivators. It will become your internal goal, and, since you've announced it, a measurable goal that others can know about. Then, if you can, give yourself a score on enthusiasm, using a 1 to represent discouragement, and 10 to represent your willingness to keep going. 10's get the brass ring!

Take the rest of the day off after you've reflected on the "why" and written it down for later review. Give yourself a reward, a really creative reward.

---

Get more done with less stress. Do it by allotting your time in increments that promote efficiency. Here's how:

Start a 25-minute work, five-minute break cycle. Set aside a 25-minute interval during which you work only on a single task. Refuse to be distracted by anything or anyone during this 25-minute time block.

When your 25 minutes are used up, rest your mind for five minutes. When five minutes are up, start your next 25-minute period.

The split is 25 and 5. The 25-minute intervals keep your attention on the task at hand, limiting the number of disruptions of your focus and flow. The five-minute break helps refresh your mind in preparation for the next 25-minute focus time.

This is science, believe me.

## Chapter 15
### WHY?
### WHAT IS YOUR MOTIVATION?

**I want my memory to be spectacular! And I want it as soon as possible!**

How badly do you want your memory to be spectacular? How motivated are you? Psychologists have come up with a method to determine whether your motivation comes from outside (extrinsic) forces or inside (intrinsic). The value of knowing this is that you can use the information to increase your motivation!

**What does motivation have to do with memory?** It's all keyed to rewards for accomplishments. Here's the rule: reward yourself when you see the memory techniques you're learning work.

At this point, you may be wondering why you've decided to pursue this study to improve your memory. After all, you're not a spring chicken any more. But, obviously, there's something inside of you that's motivating you. It's an intrinsic thing ... not brought about because of pressures from someone else. Right?

Why do you think your memory needs a little "tune-up?" You may be concerned about your recall of events or other important information. For us seniors, learning how to efficiently remember is a big step, one that most of us wish we had learned years ago. I suspect you are intrinsically motivated now and willing to commit to a program that requires some sweat equity from you.

You probably already know this, but motivation is key to this memory ability you want to acquire. What follows is a short primer that is intended to prepare you for the positive changes to come as you learn new memory skills. Don't skip this; you'll be picking up information that you can easily work into a cocktail conversation. You'll impress everyone with your understanding of how behavior is changed by outside events (extrinsic motivation) or from inside (intrinsic) needs.

**Extrinsic Motivation** refers to behavior that is driven by a desire to gain external rewards such as money, fame, grades, praise, or to avoid an adverse outcome. That's probably **not** why you are continuing to work to improve your memory. These are not typical reasons for a person your age. As a senior, you're not:

> Doing whatever is necessary to get a good performance report.
>
> Responding to a reprimand for your inactivity.
>
> Participating in a sport just to win awards.
>
> Competing in a contest to win a prize.
>
> Studying because you want to impress your book club.
>
> Cleaning your house because you have guests coming over. (This may be something you'd do!)
>
> Participating in a sports league.
>
> Competing in a contest because you know you're better than the other competitors.
>
> Proving to a companion you've still "got it." (Maybe you're still working on this one!)

In each of the above examples, an extrinsic desire motivates behavior to gain a reward or avoid an unpleasant outcome.

Memory improvement is not ordinarily extrinsically motivated.

Think of being extrinsically motivated by a desire to gain an obvious reward or avoid an adverse outcome.

**Intrinsic Motivation** typically involves an activity that is personally rewarding. This memory program is just that. Intrinsic motivation means doing something for your own self rather than for some external reward. Here are some examples of intrinsic rewards:

> Losing weight.
>
> Participating in a sport because you find the activity enjoyable.
>
> Solving a word puzzle because you find the challenge fun and exciting.

> Improving your ability to remember many things.
>
> Making a speech without having to refer to notes.

In each of these instances, your behavior is motivated by an internal desire to participate in an activity for its own sake.

**Extrinsic vs. Intrinsic Motivation: Which Is best?**

The primary differences between the two types of motivation:

> Extrinsic motivation arises from outside of the individual, while
>
> Intrinsic motivation arises from within.

It makes sense that the type of motivation can determine behavioral effectiveness. But be careful. Taking excessive external rewards for an already internally rewarding behavior can lead to a reduction in intrinsic motivation. This is the phenomenon known as the "over justification effect." (One glass of wine "reward" is enough!)

Both extrinsic and intrinsic motivation play a significant role in learning. An emphasis on external rewards (such as a night out, the purchase of a new something, or a big "Atta boy!") may undermine intrinsic motivation. However, extrinsic motivators probably contribute towards a feeling of competence, thus enhancing intrinsic motivation.

Your intrinsic interest often survives when a reward is used to signal a job well done (as in a "most improved bridge player" award). If a reward boosts feelings of competence after doing good work, enjoyment of the task may increase. Rewards, rightly administered, can motivate high performance and creativity.

> Extrinsic motivation can be beneficial in some situations:
>
> External rewards can induce interest and participation in something in which you had no initial interest (for example, you discover some of the memory techniques are fun and you are learning!).

Extrinsic rewards (like being able to remember names and faces) can motivate you to acquire new skills or knowledge.

Extrinsic rewards can also be a source of feedback, allowing you to know when your performance has achieved a standard deserving of reinforcement. (For example, at home after a big event, you're able to remember the names of people you met **and** the major points the speaker made! Have an extra piece of cake.)

Avoid extrinsic motivation in situations where:
You already find the activity intrinsically rewarding.
Being offered a reward might make a "play" activity seem more like "work."

**Intrinsic motivation is probably best,** but not always possible in every situation. Here are three conclusions about extrinsic rewards and their influence on intrinsic motivation:

**Unexpected external rewards typically do not decrease intrinsic motivation.** For example, if you were able to remember 10 peg words on your first try (you don't know how you did it, but it was pretty neat!) and your companion gives you an external reward by taking you to your favorite pizza place. Your underlying motivation for learning about the subject will not be affected. (Just don't expect such a reward every time you remember all the stuff on the first try!)

**Praise can increase internal motivation.** Offering positive praise and feedback when you do something better in comparison to others can improve intrinsic motivation.

**Intrinsic motivation will decrease, however, when external rewards are given for only doing minimal work.** For example, if your family lavishly praises you every time you complete a simple task, you'll be less intrinsically motivated to perform that task in the future.

Extrinsic and intrinsic motivation do play a significant role in learning memory techniques. Any extrinsic motivators that aid performance can't be bad. A person's interest survives when a reward neither bribes nor controls, but signals a job well done. If a reward boosts your feeling of competence for doing good work, your enjoyment of the task may increase.

*Congratulations! You've read through a chapter that isn't very interesting. Give yourself an extrinsic reward. Buy something. Have dinner out tonight.*

---

There are powerful relaxing and refreshing forces working for you: a healthy and religious attitude, good sleep, music, and laughter. Have faith in your religion, learn to sleep well, love good music, and see the fun side of life. You can do this even though we are all basically self-interested and whatever we do, we naturally expect something in return.

Be grateful to those who stand by you.

You can derive great internal satisfaction and happiness by doing good for others. Don't expect anything in return but the warm glow of contentment.

# Chapter 16
## LEARNER TYPES
## Part 1 of 2

The kind of learner you are defines the way you will best remember things. Take a look; which type of learner do you think you are?

| Learner characteristics | You're a |
|---|---|
| 1. Like words? | Linguistic Learner |
| 2. Ask lots of questions? | Logical/Mathematical Learner |
| 3. Easily visualize issues? | Spatial Learner |
| 4. Music's your thing? | Music Lover Learner |
| 5. You learn through discovery, by doing before initiating action | Body/Kinesthetic Learner |
| 6. Easily socialize with others? | Interpersonal Learner |
| 7. Like to work independently? | Intrapersonal Learner |
| 8. Love nature? | Naturalist Learner |

It's possible to be more than one type learner. However, one type will always dominate the other. There are different ways to learn; you know that. In fact, you probably know someone who learns things in a way you can't comprehend.

Remember the type of learner you are. There's more about your wonderful mind in the next chapter. As you see what the various learner types like to do, what they're good at, and how they learn best, you may understand why you're the type learner you are.

---

You are not too old! There are three ages, chronological (calculated on your date of birth), biological (determined by your health), and psychological (how old you feel you are). While you don't have control over the first, you can take care of your health with good diet and exercise. A positive and cheerful attitude and optimistic style can keep the third age at bay.

# Chapter 17
## LEARNER TYPES
## Part 2 of 2

| Learner Type | You Like to | Are Good At | Learn best |
|---|---|---|---|
| LINGUISTIC | Read, write, tell stories | Memorizing names, dates, places, trivia | Saying, hearing, and seeing words |
| LOGICAL/ MATHEMATICAL | Conduct experiments, figure things out, work with numbers, ask questions, explore patterns and relationships | Math, reasoning, logic, problem solving | Categorizing, classifying, working with abstract patterns and relationships |
| SPATIAL | Draw, build, design, create, day-dream, look at pictures, watch movies, play with machines | Imagining, sensing things, solving mazes and puzzles, reading maps and charts | Visualizing, dreaming, using the mind's eye, working with color and pictures |
| MUSIC LOVER | Sing, hum tunes, listen to music, play an instrument, respond to music | Picking up sounds, remembering melodies, noticing pitches and rhythms, keeping time | Working with rhythms, picking up the melody, reacting to the music |
| BODY/ KINESTHETIC | Move around, touch, talk, use body language | Physical activities, sports, dancing, acting, crafts | Touching, moving, interacting with space, processing knowledge through body sensations |
| INTRAPERSONAL | Have many friends, talk to people, join groups | Understanding people, leading others, organizing, communicating, manipulating, mediating conflicts | Sharing, comparing, relating, cooperating interviewing |
| INTERPERSONAL | Work alone, pursue own interests | Understanding self, focusing inward on feelings and dreams, following instincts, pursuing interests and goals, being original | Working alone, individualized projects, having own space |
| NATURALIST | Conduct observations, respond to patterns in nature | Exploring natural phenomena, seeing connections, seeing patterns, reflective thinking | Thrive in outdoors environments where you can feel things and be active participants in activities |

*The chart on the previous page is based on the work of Howard Gardner of Harvard. He wrote about the concept of Multiple Intelligences in 1983. He documents the extent to which individuals possess different kinds of minds and therefore learn, remember, perform, and understand in different ways. Subsequent studies suggest there may be additional learner types.*

A reasonable conclusion must be that you can't be everything. Take what you are and make the most of it. Don't be envious of others' abilities. Use your abilities and make the world a better place.

**Now, on to a super memory!**

---

Your present relationship is worth improving. Make a conscious decision together to step it up, try some things that may be new and out of your comfort zone. The result could be the qualitative change you've been looking for. **Here's how:**

    **Step 1: Make a commitment together to work on your relationship** and improve it. The commitment will go a long way to help you do it.

    **Step 2: Spend time together.** Healthy relationships change the way our brains work. Maintaining or creating a healthy relationship is a wise priority. Start by actually being together.

    **Step 3: Make your needs a priority**, even if that means you feel selfish. Express your needs to your partner. If your needs are not met, you'll experience feelings of disappointment, hurt and resentment. But it's up to you to be clear what your needs are. Far too many people squelch, ignore, or try to deny their needs. Science shows that to be our best we actually need safe and secure connections in our lives.

    **Step 4: Be grateful.** Increasing expressions of gratitude and appreciation creates a stronger relationship. If you see something you like, say something about it. Do not take for granted the belief that your partner knows how you feel. Everyone needs to hear on a regular basis how much they are valued and appreciated. No one needs to hear this more from you than your partner. Keep the positive interactions flowing.

## Chapter 18
### Jump On The Bandwagon!

The "bandwagon effect" refers to the tendency you and I have to conform to the behavior, style, beliefs, remembrances, or attitudes of our friends because "everyone else is doing it." The memories of our friends influence our recall of past events. That's probably one of the major reasons you want to improve your memory!

"Jump on the bandwagon" is one of a large group of cognitive biases. Cognitive biases *are errors in thinking that influence judgments and the decisions groups of people make.* This "herd instinct" influences you and other seniors more than you'd guess. Your senior social group's beliefs about aging are referred to as a "group norm."

Cognitive biases help you come to a decision quickly because your "group" has already thought it through. However, cognitive biases often introduce, intentionally or accidentally, miscalculations, mistakes, and forgetfulness.

It should come as no surprise that you and I are highly influenced by group norms. When it seems the majority of our friends are doing a certain "thing," *not* doing that "thing" becomes increasingly difficult. We want to be "like" and "behave" as our friends do. This "bandwagon" pressure can impact on what we think, what we wear, what we remember, or who we vote for. We get on the bandwagon because we want to be on the winning side. If everyone else is doing something, we are left with the impression that it is the correct thing to do. It's essentially groupthink.

Fear of exclusion also plays a role in the bandwagon effect. You don't want to be the odd one out, so going along with what the rest of the group is doing is a way to ensure inclusion and social acceptance. The need to belong, to gain acceptance and approval, pressures us to adopt group norms and attitudes of the majority. This is the bandwagon effect.

The bandwagon effect can be very powerful and lead to the ready formation and acceptance of trends. But group allegiances also tend to be fragile. People jump on the bandwagon quickly, but they also jump off it just as fast.

So, when negative ideas begin to take hold (such as "I can't remember anything and all my friends say they have the same problem!"), bandwagon beliefs can lead to serious and damaging consequences.

But, luckily, the bandwagon effect can also lead to the adoption of healthy behaviors (like not smoking).

When you become one of many people who embrace healthy choices (such as exercising), congratulations. Jumping on the bandwagon was the right choice.

*Do you see where we're going with this information?* **All this relates to memory.** Don't let anyone in your circle of friends or any prejudices (such as your age) make you think you can't improve your memory skills. You can.

Age, your arthritis, friends' problems, your heritage, what everyone else is doing ... **nothing** should keep you from enjoying life **and** being able to remember it. Get on *the memory bandwagon!*

---

Money can't buy happiness, so they say. The extraordinarily wealthy aren't significantly happier than the rest of us. That's good news I guess. The difference that money makes seems to be pretty small if we have enough to take care of "needs," a few "wants," and have a little left over to help others. Knowing how and when to spend your money **will**, in fact, buy you some happiness. A better memory **can** help. Surprised?

# Chapter 19
## Why Do We Forget?
### (Part 1 of 3)

Why do we forget? This has got to be one of seniors' most serious concerns. From forgetting where you left your keys, to forgetting to return a phone call, to being unable to remember the details of critical information, the fear of forgetting is a daily concern.

Frantically searching for missing car keys, you may think where you left your keys is permanently gone from your memory. Not true. Forgetting typically is a failure in memory **retrieval.** The information is somewhere in your head, but can't be retrieved at the moment you want it.

### The Ebbinghaus Forgetting Curve

Psychologist Hermann Ebbinghaus was one of the first to scientifically study forgetting. His published findings (in 1885) illustrated what is known as the "Ebbinghaus Forgetting Curve." He showed that we quickly forget "some" of new information, but that forgetting slows over time. The important thing he demonstrated was that there is a relationship between forgetting and time.

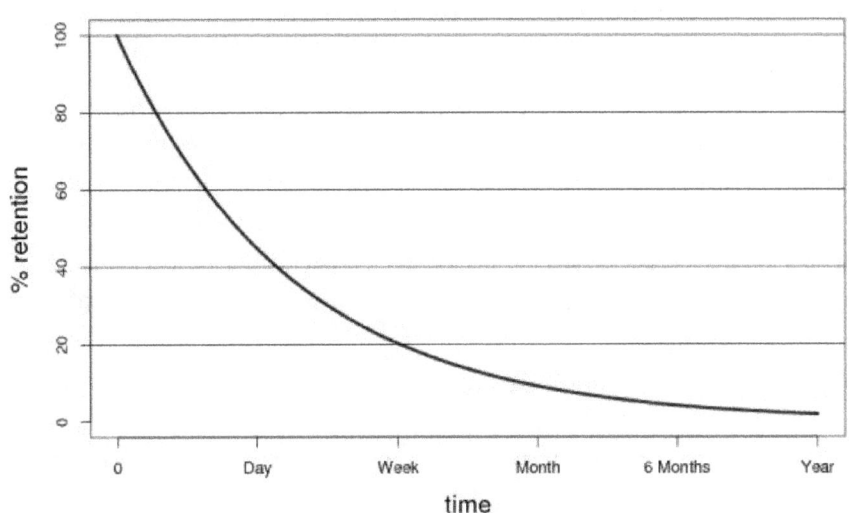

It's quite common to forget information very quickly after it is learned. However, the forgetting curve shows that forgetting does not continue to decline until all the information is lost. At a certain point, forgetting levels off, indicating that information stored in long-term memory is surprisingly stable ... somewhere. Your challenge is to have a way to retrieve what's stored in your brain.

When you're standing in the rain, frantically searching for your car keys, you're not interested in a scientific explanation of why you forgot where the keys are. But scientists **are** concerned. They know the information is in your head and that getting it into your consciousness is the challenge. Their work starts with measuring how much we can remember and what we forget. There are two good measurements that will end up with a score:

**Recall**

Memorize something, such as a list of terms, and then later recall the list from memory. What is recalled (remembered), is a measure, a score.

**Recognition**

The second method is identifying from varying amounts of information that which was previously learned. What is recognized can be measured. There will be a score.

Whether it is an occasional problem or symptom of a major style-of-living change, forgetting is a major concern to seniors. Many of us obsess over it. It may not be helpful, but there are scientific explanations why forgetting occurs. But that's not the kind of learning you're looking for. You want to remember! You've started opening your mind to new information and you will soon be learning techniques that will enhance your memory. You'll kiss forgetting goodbye!

Here are the theories generally accepted as reasons for forgetting (undoubtedly, someone will come up with more explanations as we increase our knowledge of the mind!):

Reasons for Forgetting Theeories
- **Interference**
- **Trace Decay**
- **Retrieval Failure**
- **Clue-Dependency**

These theories may be of no interest to you. If that's the case, skip the next two sessions and start by reading the chapter about taking a nap!

---

"These are the times of fast foods and slow digestion, big men and small character, steep profits and shallow relationships. These are the days of two incomes but more divorce, fancier houses but broken homes. These are days of quick trips, disposable diapers, throwaway morality, one night stands, overweight bodies, and pills that do everything from cheer, to quiet, to kill.

"A time when technology can bring a letter to you, and a time when you can choose either to share this insight, or to just hit delete.

"Remember to say, 'I love you' to your partner and your loved ones, but most of all, mean it. An embrace will mend hurt when it comes from deep inside of you.

"Life is not measured by the number of breaths we take, but by the moments that take our breath away."

Attributed to George Carlin, but written by Dr. Bob Moorehead, former pastor of Seattle's Overlake Christian Church, under the title "The Paradox of Our Age" in Words Aptly Spoken, 1995.

# Chapter 20
## WHY DO WE FORGET?
### (Part 2 of 3)

Many factors contribute to forgetting. Here are four currently accepted explanations for why forgetting occurs:

### 1. Interference

What did you have for dinner Tuesday night of last week? Is that difficult to recall? If someone had asked you that question Wednesday morning you probably would have had no problem recalling what you had for dinner the night before. But as intervening days pass, the memories of all the other meals eaten since then start to interfere with the memory of that one particular meal. This is an example of the interference theory of forgetting.

The interference theory illustrates the result of different memories interfering with one another. It is difficult to remember what happened on an average day two months ago, because so many other days have interfered since then.

It is also more likely interference will occur the more similar two or more events are to one another. However, unique and distinctive events are less likely to suffer from interference. Your senior prom, graduation, wedding, or birth of a first child are much more likely to be recalled because they are singular events, days like no other.

Interference also plays a role in what is known as the **serial position effect,** or the tendency to recall the first and last items of a list. For example, imagine you wrote a shopping list but forgot to take it with you to the store. You will probably be able to easily recall the first and last items on your list, but you might forget many of the items that were in the middle. The first thing you wrote down and the last thing you wrote down stand out as being more distinct, while the fourth item and seventh item might seem so similar they interfere with each other.

**Retroactive interference** happens when *newly acquired information interferes with old memories.* For example, a teacher learning the names of her new class of students at the start of a school year might find it more difficult to recall the names of the students in her class last year. The new information interferes with the old information.

**Proactive interference** occurs when previously *learned information makes it more difficult to form new memories.* Learning a new phone number might be more difficult, for example, because memories of the old phone number interfere with the new information.

**Eliminating interference altogether is impossible,** but there are a few things that can minimize its effects:

> **Overlearning,** which involves rehearsing the material repeatedly until it can be reproduced perfectly with no errors.
>
> **Vary routine and avoid studying similar material back to back.** For example, don't do a Rosetta Stone Spanish language study right after studying German terms. Break up similar material and switch to an intervening subject each study session.
>
> **Sleep** also plays an essential role in memory formation. Sleeping after learning something new is one of the best ways to turn new memories into lasting ones.

### 2. Trace Decay

According to the *trace decay theory,* the formation of new memories makes physical and chemical changes in the brain that result in a memory "trace." Information in short term memory lasts approximately 15 to 30 seconds, and if not rehearsed, the memory trace quickly decays.

The theory suggests that **events** that happen between the formation of a memory and the recall of the memory have little impact on recall. **It is the length of time between**

**memory formation and its recall that determines whether the information will be retained or forgotten.** If the time interval before recall is short, more information will be recalled. If a longer period of time passes, more information will be forgotten and memory will be poorer. Listening to a speech and recalling the speech is an example of trace decay.

After being exposed to new information, there may be hundreds of unique and individual decay experiences between learning the information and having to recall it. Was forgetting the date the American Revolutionary War began due to the length of time between learning the date and using the information in your book study's extemporaneous speech, or did the multitude of other information acquired during that interval of time play a role?

It's nearly impossible to eliminate all the new information that influence the creation of the memory and its recall.

A problem with the decay theory is it does not account for why some memories **fade so quickly** while others linger. Novelty is one factor. For example, a person is more likely to remember the very first day of a new job than all the intervening days between it and retirement. That first day was new and exciting, but all the following days probably seem quite similar to each other.

*The third and fourth explanations of why we forget will be covered in the next chapter.*

---

Music has the ability to change one's mood, which makes it an excellent stress reliever. In fact, music has been used therapeutically in hospitals for pain management and emotional well-being. Music is linked to happiness. Researchers have found that music is correlated with lowered stress as well as feelings of joy. So, for a quick burst of happiness, hum a tune or put on your earphones and listen to your favorite artist.

# Chapter 21
## WHY DO WE FORGET?
### (Part 3 of 3)

**3. Retrieval Failure**

Sometimes the memories are there, but we just can't seem to find them. **A common reason we don't remember information is because it never made it into long term memory in the first place.**

Here's a demonstration that proves it. From memory, try to draw the back side of a penny. Once done, compare your drawing to an actual penny.

Surprised by how poorly you recalled what the back of a penny looks like? While you had a good idea about the overall shape and color, the actual details were probably pretty fuzzy. Why? Since you don't actually need to know what the back of a penny looks like to differentiate it from other coins, you only focus on the information you do need: the overall size, shape, and color of the coin. You aren't able to retrieve what the back of a penny looks like because that information was never really encoded into your memory in the first place.

**4. Clue-Dependent**

Sometimes information is actually present in memory, but can't be recalled without retrieval clues. These clues are elements that were present at the time the actual memory was encoded. For example, guys might easier remember details of the first date with their spouse if they smell the same scent of the perfume she was wearing on that first date. The retrieval clue (the perfume) was present when that memory was created, so smelling it again can trigger the retrieval of those memories.

One effective clue-dependent technique you've probably been using all your life is known as **elaborate rehearsal.** An example would be to read the definition of a key term, study the definition of that term and then read a more detailed description of what the term means. After repeating this process a few times, recalling the information is much easier.

## In Conclusion

Coming up with answers that explain how and why we forget is a job for professionals. However, you do know:

> The passage of time makes memories more difficult to access (retrieve).
>
> The abundance of information vying for our attention creates competition between old and new memories (interference).
>
> There are times when we don't have a "clue" where the information is stored because we didn't take the time to recall the memory after it was created. So, it disappeared!

### *Cue and Clue*

> *A cue is anything said or done that serves as a signal to begin a speech or performance.*
>
> *A clue is anything that serves to lead to the solution of a problem, mystery, etc.*
>
> *A clue is part of the evidence of a past happening; a cue is a signal for a future beginning.*
>
> *Memory uses both.*

Reference authors: Cherry, K. A. is the major reference **author**. Also, Brown, John (1958), Hunt, R. R., & Worthen, J. B. (2006), Nickerson, R. S., & Adams, M. J. (1979), Tulving, E. (1974), and Willingham, D. T. (2007).

---

Show appreciation and gratitude for the little things. My wife often makes me a cup of coffee, and I always make a point of thanking her, which she, embarrassed, always dismisses. But she always smiles, because she knows I appreciate her kindness. Then when I make her morning coffee, the same thing happens - she thanks me and I dismiss her saying it's nothing. But I really love to hear her thank me, and see her smile - knowing she knows I love her.

# Chapter 22
## TAKE A NAP--IT WILL IMPROVE YOUR MEMORY

Relax. When you're relaxed it's easier to focus on things you want to remember.

Relax. Take a **short** nap, about 20-30 minutes.

Napping can increase your productivity, enabling you to become more creative. Napping puts the body in a relaxed state, which counteracts the effects of daily stress. Isn't that great information?

Although sleep comes in five stages, if your nap only takes you from Stage 1 sleep (just drifting off) to Stage 2 (brain activity slows), you will wake up feeling energized and more alert.

*Sleep Stage 1* typically lasts about 10 minutes and Sleep Stage 2 lasts another 10 minutes. That makes the 20-minute nap ideal for most people (your time will vary to some degree).

However, If your nap takes you into stages 3 and 4 (both components of deep sleep), you will not wake easily and will feel groggy and tired. Don't do that.

**How to Nap Effectively**

Each of us has our own unique nap style. The best nap is the one in which you fall asleep quickly, stay asleep for a short time, and wake refreshed. Napping too long may actually leave you feeling more tired. Here are some suggestions:

**Nap Time:** Prime nap time is from 1:00 p.m. to 3:00 p.m., when your energy level dips due to a rise in the hormone Melatonin.

**Darkness:** Use a facemask or eye pillow to provide daytime darkness.

**Not Too Late:** Don't nap within three hours of bedtime. It may interfere with nighttime sleep.

**Quiet Place:** Rest somewhere you will not be disturbed for the duration of your nap.

**30-Minute Maximum:** When taking nap longer than 30 minutes, you run the risk of heading into deep sleep, which will leave you feeling tired and groggy. Naps as short as one to two minutes may be effective for some people.

**Set an Alarm:** You will eventually train yourself to nap for the time you set aside. Until then, set your phone alarm for the nap end time, or ask someone to wake you up.

**The Caffeine Nap:** You might benefit from drinking a cup of coffee and then taking an immediate nap. The caffeine kicks in after 10 to 20 minutes, waking you up. You get extra energy from both the nap and the coffee.

I don't expect this chapter to be controversial. After all, who doesn't like a short nap?

*Sources: Naska A, Oikonomou E, Trichopoulou A, Psaltopoulou T, Trichopoulos D. Siesta in healthy adults and coronary mortality in the general population. Arch Intern Med. 2007 Feb 12;167(3):296-301. National Institutes of Health; National Heart, Lung, and Blood Institute. Your Guide to Healthy Sleep. NIH Publication No. 06-5271. Hayashi M, Masuda A, Hori T. The alerting effects of caffeine, bright light and face washing after a short daytime nap. Clinical Neurophysiology. 2003 Dec;114(12):2268-78.*

---

Artificial intelligence is no match for natural stupidity.

I'm great at multi-tasking--I can waste time, be unproductive, and procrastinate all at once.

Take my advice. I'm not using it.

Television may insult your intelligence, but nothing rubs it in like a computer.

Women sometimes make fools of men, but most guys are the do-it-yourself type.

No matter how much you push the envelope, it'll still be stationery.

## Chapter 23
### THE FIVE STAGES OF SLEEP

This chapter is just for information. Knowing about the five stages of sleep won't help much when you're staring at the ceiling, still awake an hour or so after you went to bed.

**Stage 1 Sleep**

This is the lightest stage of sleep, the *transition phase*, where you feel yourself drifting off. If you were to forget about the alarm clock and allow yourself to wake up naturally, Stage 1 sleep would also be the last stage before you fully wake up. You don't spend too much time in Stage 1 sleep, typically five to 10 minutes, just enough to allow your body to slow down and your muscles to relax.

**Stage 2 Sleep**

The second stage of sleep is still considered light sleep. Your brain activity starts to slow down, as well as your heart rate and breathing. Your body temperature falls a little and you're beginning to reach a state of total relaxation. Stage 2 sleep is in preparation for the deeper sleep to come.

**Stage 3 Sleep**

Stage 3 sleep is the start of deep sleep, also known as slow wave sleep. During Stage 3 your brain waves are slow "delta waves," although there may still be short bursts of faster brain activity (known as "beta-waves"). If you were to get awakened suddenly during this stage, you would be groggy and confused, and find it difficult at first to focus.

**Stage 4 Sleep**

Of the five stages of sleep, it is in Stage 4 you will experience your deepest sleep. Your brain only shows slow wave activity in Stage 4 and it's difficult to wake someone up when they're in this stage. Although stages 3 and 4 can last anywhere from 5 to 15 minutes each, Stage 4 sleep will probably last an hour or so. This is the time when the body does most of its repair work and regeneration.

**Stage 5 Sleep**

This is the dream stage of sleep. It is referred to as "active sleep" or REM sleep (which stands for the rapid eye movements that characterize Stage 5 sleep). During REM sleep, your blood flow, breathing, and brain activity increase. An EEG would show that your brain is about as active as it is when you're awake.

An interesting characteristic of Stage 5 sleep is that the muscles in your arms and legs will go through periods of paralysis. Scientists speculate that this may be nature's way of protecting us from acting out our dreams.

The first period of active Stage 5 REM sleep usually begins about 90 minutes after you start drifting off, and lasts for about 10 minutes. As the night passes, the periods of REM sleep become longer, with the final episode lasting an hour or so. Babies may spend as much as half of the time they're asleep in the REM phase. For a healthy adult, Stage 5 sleep occurs about 20 to 25% of the time spent sleeping, and decreases with age.

---

**Life** is too short to wake up with regrets. Life is filled with memories, but no one looks back on their life and remembers the nights they had plenty of sleep. Life is filled with good memories of people.

Love the people who treat you right. Forget about the ones who don't. Be thankful for what you have. Don't wait until it's too late to tell someone how much you love them and how much you care about them, because when you or they are gone, no matter how much we shout and cry, they won't hear you anymore.

## Chapter 24
### Evaluating Memory

You can put anything into your memory. Truth and fiction both reside there.

So how do you know whether the things you remember are accurate? Do you sometimes make your "recall" what you want it to be rather than how it was? You can do that.

If someone does a fact check on your story, they might discover some past events really happened (their occurrence can be objectively verified), and some things can't be checked for accuracy (your imagination is great!).

Memory is either verifiable or it's not. The memory test is whether our recall is what we want it to be, or what the past really was. It's either an unverified recollection or a checkable memory. One or the other; subjective or objective. (Here are those words again!) Back in Chapter 11 we defined the terms:

> **Subjective memory** is your perception of the past. Subjective memory is not measurable.
>
> **Objective memory** can be measured. Objective evaluation results in a "score."

Objective memory counts. You're learning how to remember. What you remember is another story.

For the record, you're in control. You're on your way to becoming a Memory Whiz!

---

"A human being is a part of a whole, called by us universe, a part limited in time and space. He experiences himself, his thoughts and feelings, as something separated from the rest... a kind of optical delusion of his consciousness. This delusion is a kind of prison for us, restricting us to our personal desires and to affection for a few persons nearest to us. Our task must be to free ourselves from this prison by widening our circle of compassion to embrace all living creatures and the whole of nature in its beauty." Albert Einstein

# SECTION TWO

## Chapter 25
### WHAT'S NEXT?

Starting with this chapter, you'll be reading a lot about the five techniques I think will be of most value to you in the years ahead. There will be descriptions and "how to" explanations of other techniques, but they won't get the emphasis these five will.

Here are the five techniques I feel are of most value to seniors:

Peg Words

Mnemonics

Keyword

Memory Palace

Links

You'll read about these techniques as ways to remember names and faces, things, numbers, and word for word retention. The techniques can be applied to any situation. Honest!

If you skipped the first section of the book and your first exposure to memory techniques is starting with this chapter, this is where we get to the specifics. (If you're starting in this section, I do think you've missed a lot of the "happy hour" information that adds a bit of color to learning. The first section is a distillation of the best information I could lay my hands on, plus my own suggestions -- a combination that has helped many people just like you.)

Scientists and scholars have identified lots of ways people forget. More importantly, many techniques have been developed to help seniors remember current and past events. There are some really great suggestions waiting on the pages ahead. One or more of them will be just what you've been looking for.

---

We are all basically self-interested. Whatever we do, we naturally expect something in return. We should definitely be grateful to those who stood by us. But our focus should be on the internal satisfaction and happiness we derive by doing good for others, without expecting anything in return but the warm glow we get, which in the end, is what we really want.

## Chapter 26
### THE TWO-STEP PROCESS TO MAKE A MEMORY

Making a memory requires just two steps:

The memory **and**

The place in your head where you put it.

This section includes information on the critical parts of the two-step process.

It's important stuff. You'll be getting the "nuts and bolts" of memory, written so you can absorb the information relatively easily. But, as you already know, there is a "sweat equity" to learning.

---

**Old age is when:**
  You stop growing at both ends, and begin to grow in the middle.
  You're cautioned to slow down by your doctor instead of by the police.
  Everything starts to wear out, fall out, or spread out.
    You learn that by the time you're 70, there will be five women to every man. Isn't that the darndest time for a guy to get those odds?
    You have a choice between two temptations and you choose the one that will get you home earlier.
    Caution is the only thing you care to exercise.
    "Getting a little action" means you don't need to take a laxative!

## Chapter 27
### USING YOUR MEMORY

You've got a filing cabinet in your head.

You get information from your mind in the same way you physically find documents in a filing cabinet: by looking in labeled drawers and folders you've created. The problem with remembering isn't that the information is not in your brain, it's retrieving it. The information is there, but where? Did you forget to label it?

Successful memory storage and retrieval systems use visualization, association, and substitute words as mental clues for remembering. These three words, *visualization, association, and substitution,* are, as you are discovering, very important.

The mental images you create act as pointers for the actual facts in your memory. *Image memory systems* work so well because most people can remember images better than abstract knowledge.

In pages to come are brief descriptions of the major memory systems, followed by the main descriptors you'll be learning about and, ultimately, using.

There are many ways to remember. Why so many? Because each method is useful for a different kind of information. A good analogy is a toolbox full of different tools. You wouldn't expect to use a hammer to saw boards, or a screwdriver to pound nails. To build a house, or a strong memory, you must select the right tool for the job.

---

You don't have to be great to start, but you have to start to be great. So, start this way: plan with attitude, prepare with aptitude, participate with servitude, and receive with gratitude. That will be enough to separate you from the multitudes.

**You'll be a winner** ... if you can **be big** enough to admit your mistakes, **smart** enough to profit from them, and **strong** enough to correct them!.

## Chapter 28
### Memory Vocabulary

Following are the terms memory professionals use when discussing their profession. You should be familiar with all of them. This is your first exposure; you'll be seeing these important terms many more times.

| ACRONYMS | An acronym is a word or expression formed from the first letters of words and pronounced as a separate word, such as **sonar** (*from <u>so</u>und <u>na</u>vigation and <u>r</u>anging*). Acronyms are used most often to abbreviate names of organizations and long or frequently referenced terms. |
|---|---|
| | Acronyms (as an expression or word) are the most popularly used memory mnemonic technique for remembering an expression or a word. |
| | **The distinguishing feature of an acronym is that it is pronounced as if it were a single word:** |
| | **NATO** is an acronym for the North Atlantic Treaty Organization. |
| | **NASA** is an acronym for the National Aeronautics and Space Administration (USA). |
| | **FANBOYS** is an acronym for the English language's seven coordinating conjunctions (**f**or, **a**nd, **n**or, **b**ut, **o**r, **y**et, **s**o). |
| | **ASAP** stands for *"as soon as possible."* This acronym is used when someone is asked to do something quickly: "Send me the report ASAP." *(Interestingly, "ASAP" is also an abbreviation when pronounced using each letter, A.S.A.P.).* |
| | Acronyms aid memorization but not necessarily comprehension. |

What's the difference between an **acronym** and an **abbreviation?**

An **acronym** is a word or name formed from the first letters of the full name or sentence and pronounced as a separate word.

An **abbreviation** is a shortened form of a word or phrase. It consists of the first letters of a longer sentence. Each letter is spelled out and not read as a word. For example, **BBC** (British Broadcasting Company) and **IBM** (International Business Machines), are both abbreviations, because each letter is pronounced.

| | |
|---|---|
| **ACROSTICS** | Acrostic mnemonics, like acronyms, use the first letter of each word, but instead of making a new word, the letters are used to make a sentence. Acrostics are especially useful for long lists of things whose names don't begin with vowels. Like acronyms, acrostics can be very simple to remember and are particularly helpful when you need to remember a list in a specific order. Here are two examples:<br><br>**My Dear Aunt Sally** (for the mathematical order of operations: Multiply and Divide before you Add and Subtract)<br><br>**King Phil Came Over for the Genes Special** (for the taxonomic hierarchy: Kingdom, Phylum, Class, Order, Genus, Species)<br><br>One advantage of acrostics over acronyms is that they are less limiting. But acrostics can take more thought to create and require remembering a whole new sentence rather than just one word (as is the case with acronyms). They also present the same problem as acronyms in that they aid memorization but not comprehension. |
| **ASSOCIATION** | The way new information can best be remembered is by consciously **associating** it with something already known or remembered. You'll read this a lot: *"Virtually all learning is based on memory. You can remember any new piece of information if it is vividly associated to something you already know or remember."* Learning how to associate new to known is the key to a trained memory. |
| **CHUNKING** | Chunking is a way to break a large group of items into subgroups. "1234567890" chunked would be "123-456-7890." This is a technique generally used to remember numbers, although chunking can be used for remembering other things as well. It is based on the idea that short-term memory is limited in the number of things that can be retained. |

| | |
|---|---|
| INTERACTION | Interaction is the association of two items and the creation of a connection between them. One of the images must be doing something to or with the other image. Each part of the unit serves as a clue for remembering the rest of the unit. |
| KEYWORD | The Keyword Method converts the sound of an unfamiliar word or object into one or more easily visualized words or objects which then become the link to the actual meaning of the word.<br><br>For example, using a keyword to distinguish between the *diameter* of a circle and the *radius* of a circle. (The "diameter" is a line from the edge-to-edge of a circle passing through the center. The "radius" is a line from the center of the circle to the edge.)<br><br>Choose radius as the keyword to distinguish between diameter and radius. Imagine a radish (the radius sound-alike word) swinging inside a circle. When "radius" is mentioned, the sound of the word will remind you of radish and the image of a radish swinging inside a circle to the circle's edge. That will be your signal that "radius" is the line from the center of the circle to the edge.<br><br>***Easy. Right?*** |
| LINK | A Link is used to remember things in sequence. One item "links" to another. Linking utilizes *substitution, out-of-proportion, exaggeration, and action*. Links that make use of the five senses are best. A link must lead from one item to the next. Linking is an important process. |

| | |
|---|---|
| **MEMORY PALACE** | The Memory Palace is a technique based on a skill each of us has: we're very good at remembering details of places we know. A "Memory Palace" is a metaphor for places you can easily visualize, like the rooms in your home and the things that are in that room.<br><br>The concept is useful for managing complex or lengthy material like a speech without notes. For a speech, each main talking point would be related to the succession of rooms or landmarks on the journey. The details associated with a main point of the speech (the location) trigger recall of related information.<br><br>Making the Memory Palace journey from one familiar spot to another is a way to store and recall all kinds of information. Using a route's memorable features as pegs and associating new information to the peg combines the techniques of **Association, Location, Imagination, Organization,** and **Visual Memory.** |
| **MIND MAP** | Mind Mapping organizes material on a subject as one thinks laterally, creatively, and randomly about it. The idea is to build a map (a picture of ideas) as they come to you, thereby establishing logical connections and sequences. |
| **MNEMONICS** | The word, *mnemonic* (the first "m" is silent), is derived from "Mnemosyne," the Greek goddess of memory. Mnemonic tools and techniques assist recall and information retention. The use of one of the nine mnemonic devices is based on the observation that *spatial, personal, surprising, physical, sexual, humorous,* or otherwise *relatable* information is more easily remembered by the mind than abstract or impersonal forms of information. Mnemonics work. |

| | |
|---|---|
| **NAMES AND FACES** | The secret to remembering **names and faces** is paying attention, really close attention. The process starts with making up a substitute name for the person's name (Daniels= Dan yells). Then choose Mr. Daniel's most prominent physical characteristic (his large ears). Finally, link the substitute name (Dan yells) and the physical characteristic together in an image that is funny, strange, ridiculous, etc. (See Dan yelling into a giant ear.) When you next see him and his big ears, you'll imagine this ridiculous picture and remember "Daniels." |
| **NOTE ORGANIZATION** | Organized notes can promote learning and recall; in this respect, notes are a memory device. |
| **NUMBERS** | Knowing how to remember **numbers** is an important skill since so much of everyday life involves numbers. Convert numbers to words (it's a lot easier to remember words). Use peg words for the conversion method. Find each number's peg letter equivalent and then either put all the consonants together and add vowels to make word(s) or make each consonant the beginning letter of words in a sentence. Either way works. |
| **OBJECTIVE MEMORY** | An objective indicator of memory performance is a way that can be measured. Being able to establish a comparative score for anything is important. Objective memory is better than subjective memory. |
| **PEG** | A peg system is a way to remember phone numbers, addresses, numerical sequences, or lists, by visualizing objects and pairing them with a peg (usually an object that can be recalled in a numbered sequence).<br><br>Use pegging to establish location in a numbered list. Thoughts are tied to a tangible image of a number (for example, 1=tie), and thus able to be recalled at specific points.<br><br>**Pegging is a good system for seniors.** |

| | |
|---|---|
| **PEG WORDS** | Using peg letters, numbers are converted into consonant sounds. then into **peg words** by adding vowels and non-counting consonants, and finally, to images that can be associated with the word or picture to be remembered. Each peg number is represented by a word using one or more consonants.<br><br>For example, in a peg word system:<br><br>The number "2" is represented by the letter "n." The "n" converted to a peg word becomes "**Noah**," created using as fillers o, a, and h from the non-counting vowels (a, e, i, o, u), and non-counting consonants (w, h, y, and x).<br><br>Associate *Noah* with the word (or picture) you want to remember. (Imagine the second word to remember is "beer.") See Noah walking onto the ark with 2 kegs of Budweiser under his arms. Then, when someone says "2" or "Noah," you'll remember the kegs of beer<br><br>The number "6" is represented either by **j, sh, ch,** and the **soft g.** Using the **"sh"** plus non-counting vowels, the **"sh"** is converted to the peg word "**Shoe.**" |
| **PHONETIC ALPHABET** | The phonetic **alphabet** uses symbols to represent individual sounds in written form. |
| **RECALL WORD-FOR-WORD** | To remember word-for-word, or verbatim, the subject matter is repeated word-for-word when compared with the original document. The best technique for memorizing is **recall,** as opposed to rote memorization. **Recall creates a new brain connection,** strengthening the same brain pathways that will be activated when the information is used again. The technique is not rote memorization. |

| | |
|---|---|
| RHYME | Rhyme, repetition, melody, and rhythm can all aid memory. Are you familiar with Homer's Odyssey? It's quite long. That is why it is so remarkable to realize that this story was told by storytellers who would rely solely on their memories. The use of rhyme, rhythm, and repetition helped the storytellers remember.<br><br>The same techniques can be used to better remember information. Even the simple addition of a familiar rhythm and melody can help. Many children learn the letters of the alphabet to the tune of "Twinkle, Twinkle, Little Star." Rhymes draw on your auditory memory and may be particularly useful for those who can learn tunes, songs, or poems easily. |
| SPELLING | Examples of Spelling techniques:<br>A princi**pal** at a school is your **pal,** and a princip**le** you believe or follow is a ru**le**.<br>To spell "Saskatchewan" : **A**sk **A**t **C**hew **A**n with an **S** in front of it. (Wow!) |
| SUBJECTIVE MEMORY | Subjective memory represents the perception of memory performance. Subjective memory is **not** measurable.<br>Objective memory is better. |
| VISUALIZATION | Visualization is the joining of images together in an outlandish manner. Visualization enables a new visual image to be associated to an image already stored in the brain. Visualized images must be joined; side-by-side doesn't work. It's best to substitute and integrate images into the most bizarre and graphic way you can think of. Substitution, Visualization, and Association work together to create recallable memories. |

Have you noticed the many strings of words used in the explanations? Their use illustrates the importance of associations and combinations in memorization. Here are some string examples:

> Association, location, imagination, organization, and visual memory
>
> Names, dates, facts, figures, pictures, letters, rhymes, words, songs, steps, stages, parts, and phases
>
> Personal, surprising, physical, sexual, humorous, spatial, or other "relatable" information
>
> Phone numbers, addresses, numerical sequences, or lists
>
> Rhyme, melody, rhythm, and repetition
>
> Ridiculous, wild, out of proportion, extravagant, in a huge quantity, is reminiscent of, or sounds like
>
> Spatial, personal, surprising, physical, sexual, or humorous
>
> Steps, stages, parts, phases
>
> Substitution, out of proportion, exaggeration, and action

*[The sources for most of the definitions in this chapter: The Brilliant Memory Book (Dominic O'Brien); Memory Book (Harry Lorayne and Jerry Lucas); Achieving Optimal Memory (Arron Nelson and Gary Small), The Memory Bible (Aaron P. Nelson), Your Memory (Kenneth B. Higbee), Ageless Memory (Harry Lorayne), and Moonwalking with Einstein (Joshua Foer). Of course, there are many other authors.]*

---

We of a certain age have been blessed to live in changeful times. For a child, each new word is like a shiny toy, a toy that has no age. Those of us a little older have the advantage of remembering there are words that once did not exist, that strutted upon the earthly stage and now are heard no more, except in our collective memory. It's one of the great advantages of aging.

## Chapter 29
### MEMORY MNEMONICS

Creating a recallable memory is what it's all about.
Putting it into your head is easy.
***Getting it back is the challenge.***

Let's start this very important section with a quick introduction to mnemonics, a memory technique. (This part starts out with a little more detail than usual, but hang in there, it'll all make sense!)

A mnemonic is a hypernym. A hypernym word is superior to other, lesser words. Within a hypernym are hyponyms (words of more specific meaning than the hypernym). It's easier to understand the concept by looking at an example.

| *Hypernym* | Cutlery |
|---|---|
| *Hyponym* | Knife |

Hyponyms can go lower and lower into other levels of a hypernym. In doing so, they become hypernyms. For example, Spoon was a hyponym of Cutlery. Looking to the many types of spoons, the process starts over, with spoon becoming the hypernym.

| *Hypernym* | Spoon | |
|---|---|---|
| *Hyponym* | Teaspoon | Soup Spoon |

Hypernyms and hyponyms are asymmetric, meaning they are unbalanced. There are more hyponyms than hypernyms.

Almost any physical idea (hypernym) can be broken down into smaller parts or subsystems (hyponyms). A hyponym shares a relationship to its hypernym. For example, pigeon, crow, eagle, and seagull are all hyponyms of bird (their hypernym).

Hyponymy can be tested by substituting X and Y in the sentence, "X is a kind of Y," and determining if it makes sense. For example, "A screwdriver is a kind of tool" (the hypernym) makes sense, but not, "A tool is a kind of screwdriver."

What does this have to do with memory? **Group like things together.** It makes them make sense and easier to remember. **Categorize them.** That means group like things together in a structured manner. Grouped together, words become part of something larger ... they become related to one another and connected in a logical, meaningful order. Both tangible and intangible items or ideas can usually be grouped together by a common link. Linked, they are easier to remember.

Some practical examples:

Menus, where items are presented in categories such as appetizers, beverages, main entrees, desserts.

Bookstore, where books are displayed by category, such as gardening, cooking, computers, hobbies.

Supermarket, where food is displayed by group, such as vegetables, breads, candies.

OK, grouping "like" things together make memorizing easier. But what's a "mnemonic?" And why should I care?

A *mnemonic* (a hypernym) is an encompassing term for the various techniques that aid the retention of information in human memory. It's the **Memory Mnemonic Techniques** that do the work. (Pronounce "mnemonics" with the "m" being silent: "ne-mon-ics.")

Memory Mnemonic Techniques help internalize information so that it will be much easier to remember (retrieve). That's a good thing! Memory mnemonics graphically convert verbal or written descriptions into images the brain can better retain. The techniques use list-like characteristics such as steps, stages, parts, phases, etc., all part of a structured order. Successfully associate new information to information already locked in your long-term memory; the result will be combined memories that will last a very long time.

There are nine generally accepted types of mnemonics:
1. Music
2. Name
3. Expression/Word

4. Mode
5. Ode/Rhyme
6. Note Organization
7. Image
8. Connection
9. Spelling

Have you noticed the first letter of the types of mnemonics spells "Mnemonics?"

**M**
**N**
**E**
**M**
**O**
**N**
**I**
**C**
**S**

Memory Mnemonic Techniques are important because they translate information into a form the human brain can better retain than in its original form.

If you can, **consciously encoding new information the first time you are exposed to it makes memory creation easier.** The challenge is to find the best way to relate new information to information you already have locked in your long-term memory. When you can do that, you will be able to recall both the new and the old information.

You want to get remembered (retrievable) information when you want it. You want those memories that are in your head to be arranged in a way that when you want to tell a story, or a joke, or remember a person's name, or where your keys are, or where your car is parked, **you can retrieve them!**

That's where we're headed.

Memory Mnemonic techniques don't have to have any

connection to the material to be remembered, but **must** assist in its recall. **Visually perceive** information as personal, surprising, physical, sexual, humorous, spatial, or as another "relatable" image. Then store it away. Visually perceived information is much easier to find in your head than is abstract or impersonal data. Shoot for visual every time!

The memory mnemonic techniques described in this series assist in the recall of names, dates, facts, figures, pictures, letters, rhymes, words, songs, steps, stages, parts, and phases ... everything. (If there's something left out, sorry.) The process starts by storing information away in one of two ways:

Visually through the senses in associations that relate to the ability to see, hear, or become aware of something, or

Verbally by making associations with words.

**Visual associations are best,** but both visual and verbal techniques create meaningful associations with what is new to what is already known.

You're who you are today because of your memory. You can become a memory whiz when you understand memory mnemonics and start using its many techniques.

That's enough for this session. Don't leave until you're comfortable with the names of the nine types of mnemonics. They are vital keys to memory. Here they are again:

1. Music
2. Name
3. Expression/Word
4. Mode
5. Ode/Rhyme
6. Note Organization
7. Image
8. Connection
9. Spelling

---

A pretty face gets old, a nice body will change. But a good woman will always be a good woman!

# Chapter 30
# MORE ON MNEMONICS

**Mnemonics** are memory devices that help in the recall of information.

Many types of mnemonics exist. Which type works best is limited only by your imagination. As mentioned in the previous chapter, the nine generally accepted types of mnemonics are **Music, Name, Expression/Word, Model, Ode/Rhyme, Note Organization, Image, Connection,** and **Spelling Mnemonics.** Each type makes it easier to remember things.

1. **Music Mnemonics**

How many lyrics to songs do you remember? How did you come to remember them? Music can help recall important details of main ideas by making songs out of information when a list of items must be learned. Advertising on radio and TV uses music to help potential customers remember their products. Some children learn the ABC's by singing the "ABC" song. Other children learn all the states in alphabetical order using the "50 Nifty United States" song.

2. **Name Mnemonics** (Acronym)

In a **Name Mnemonic,** the first letter of each word in a list of items is used to make a name of a person or thing. Sometimes, the items can be rearranged to form an easier remembered Name Mnemonic. Examples:

**POTUS** = The **P**resident **o**f **t**he **U**nited **S**tates.

**ROY G. BIV** = colors of the spectrum (**R**ed, **O**range, **Y**ellow, **G**reen, **B**lue, **I**ndigo, **V**iolet.)

**PVT. TIM HALL** = The 10 essential amino acids (**P**henylalanine, **V**aline, **T**hreonine, **T**ryptophan, **I**soleucine, **M**ethionine, **H**istidine, **A**rginine, **L**eucine, and **Ly**sine.

3. **Expression or Word Mnemonic** (Acrostic)

This is by far the most popularly used mnemonic technique. To make an **Expression or Word** Mnemonic, the first letter of each word in a list is arranged to form a phrase or word. Examples:

> The order of operations for math, **P**arentheses, **E**xponents, **M**ultiply, **D**ivide, **A**dd, and **S**ubtract = **Please Excuse My Dear Aunt Sally**.
>
> The categories in the classification of life, **K**ingdom, **P**hylum, **C**lass, **O**rder, **F**amily, **G**enus, **S**pecies, **V**ariety = **Kings Play Cards On Fairly Good Soft Velvet**.
>
> The order of color coding on electronic resistors, **B**lack, **B**lue, **R**ed, **O**range, **Y**ellow, **G**reen, **B**rown, **V**iolet, **G**ray, **W**hite, **S**ilver, **G**old = **B**ad **B**eer **R**ots **O**ur **Y**oung **G**uts **B**ut **V**odka **G**oes **W**ell (in) **S**ilver **G**oblets.
>
> The eight small bones in the wrist, **N**avicular, **L**unate, **T**riquetrum, **P**isiform, **M**ultangular (Greater), **M**ultangular (Lesser), **C**apitate, **H**amate=**N**ever **L**ick **T**illy's **P**opsicle, **M**other **M**ight **C**ome **H**ome.
>
> At one time, the order of the planets from the sun outward was **M**ercury, **V**enus, **E**arth, **M**ars, **J**upiter, **S**aturn, **U**ranus, **N**eptune, and **P**luto= **My Very Energetic Mother Just Served Us Nine Pizzas**. (Pluto doesn't count anymore, so the new acrostic is: **My Very Evil Mother Just Served Us Newts**.)
>
> The nerves, **o**lfactory, **o**ptic, **o**culomotor, **t**rochlear, **t**rigeminal, **a**bducens, **f**acial, **a**coustic, **g**lossopharyngeal, **v**agus, **s**pinal accessory and **h**ypoglossal= "**On Old Olympus' Towering Tops, A Finn And German Viewed Some Hops**."

4. Model Mnemonics

In a **Model Mnemonic**, a graphic representation is constructed to help with understanding and recalling important information. Examples: a circular sequence model, a pyramid model of stages, a pie chart, and a 5-box sequence.

5. Ode or Rhyme Mnemonics

An **Ode or Rhyme Mnemonic** puts information in the form of a poem. Examples:

For the number of days in each month:

"**30 days hath September, April, June, and November.**

**All the rest have 31**

**Except February my dear son.**

**It has 28 and that is fine,**

**But in Leap Year it has 29."**

You'd probably prefer your doctor to know the difference between "cyanate" and "cyanide": "**Cyanate I ate** and **Cyanide I died.** Cyanide **is** a little fatal."

Remember this one? "**In 1492, Columbus sailed the ocean blue."**

6. Note Organization

The way textbook and lecture notes are organized can either inhibit learning and recall or promote it. In the sense that the organization of notes **can** promote recall, it is a memory device. Examples:

**Notecards** are an easy way to organize main ideas and relevant details. When main ideas are formatted into possible test questions, notecards can give learners practice in seeing questions and recalling answers.

**Outlines** clearly separate main ideas from details. Outlining helps organize the information in the mind, making it easier to remember.

7. Image Mnemonics

The information in an **Image Mnemonic** is in the form of a picture that promotes recall. The sillier the **Image Mnemonic,** the easier it is to recall the related information.

The images may be mental or sketched into text and notes. Examples:

Picture a limp, depressed **bat** that took the depressant drugs **B**arbiturates, **A**lcohol, and **T**ranquilizers).

Picture meeting someone new at a party named John Horsley. Use an **Image Mnemonic** to help you remember his name. Visualize a horse sitting on the "john." It's not pretty, but is effective in recall.

What is a numismatist? Visualize a new mist from the ocean rolling onto a beach of coins. Silly? Of course, but the image makes it is easier to remember that a numismatist is a coin collector.

Use a bad joke to help you remember? Picture two numismatists having a drink for "old dime's sake." Corny? Yes, but the image makes things easier to remember.

8. **Connection Mnemonics**

The information to be remembered is connected to something already known. Examples:

Remembering the direction of longitude and latitude is easier to do when you realize that lines on a globe that run North and South are long and that coincides with **LONG**itude.

9. **Spelling Mnemonics**

Examples of Spelling Mnemonics:

A princi**pal** at a school is your **pal**, and a princip**le** you believe or follow is a ru**le**.

A combination with an **Ode/Rhyme Mnemonic**--

> **I before e except after c**
>
> **or when sounding like a**
>
> **in neighbor and weigh**

In review, write the name of **each mnemonic beside its** letter:

**M**
**N**
**E**
**M**
**O**
**N**
**I**
**C**
**S**

> There is plenty of evidence showing that if you train your cognitive functions with the same determination as you train your muscles at the gym, it is possible to maintain and to improve mental fitness at an older age. The most encouraging findings show that training does not have to continue permanently as intensively as in the beginning, but cognitive training should be integrated into your lifestyle. Build a brain training habit – keep your brain fit.

## Chapter 31
### REVERSE ACRONYMS

**A reverse acronym is a mnemonic expression formed, sometimes humorously, from the letters of an** existing word or name, usually after the word or name has been in use a while. It does not define the word itself as acronyms do. (Reverse acronyms have an alternate name: *backronym,* a blend of "backwards" and "acronym.")

An example of a reverse acronym is the "Apgar" score, used to assess the health of newborn babies. The rating system was devised by and named for Virginia Apgar. However, about 10 years after the initial publication of her defining works, a backronym, Apgar, was coined as a mnemonic learning aid, rather than referencing the name of the person who created the health-scoring technique. The backronym stands for **A**ppearance, **P**ulse, **G**rimace, **A**ctivity, and **R**espiration.

Alcoholics Anonymous and other 12-step programs use backronyms as teaching tools, using slogans such as "One day at a time," or "Let go, let God." Reverse acronyms are often created using words to convey a meaning opposite to its literal meaning. For example, an alcoholic slip may be expanded as "**S**obriety **L**osing **I**ts **P**riority," and denial as "**D**on't **E**ven **N**otice **I** **A**m **L**ying."

Backronyms are also created as jokes or as slogans, often expressing consumer loyalties or frustration. For example, the name of the restaurant chain Arby's is a play on the letters "RB," referring to the company's founders, the Raffel brothers. An advertising campaign in the 1980s created a backronym slogan, "America's Roast Beef. Yes Sir!"

NASA named its ISS treadmill the Combined Operation Load-Bearing External Resistance Treadmill (C O L B E R T) after Stephen Colbert. The backronym was a lighthearted compromise in recognition of the naming of an ISS module.

Some backronyms name the subject to make obvious its purpose or characteristics. During the Iraq War, the GBU-43B Massive Ordnance Air Blast bomb (abbreviated MOAB) was a

US backed, heavily promoted backronym as the "Mother of All Bombs." This was a response to Saddam Hussein's phrase, "Mother of all battles," from the first Gulf War.

In commercial aviation, ETOPS is officially an acronym for "Extended-range Twin-engine Operational Performance Stan-dards," defining safety standards for long-distance overwater flights by planes with only two engines. But in aviation vernacular, the colloquial backronym is "Engines Turn or Passengers Swim."

*Your memory vocabulary is increasing!* **Congratulations!** *You've made another small "Kaizen" step forward! Review again the "Nine Types of Mnemonics," before you move to the next chapter.*

---

If you really love your kids and kin, taking care of yourself and your health should be your priority. Do this and you will not be a burden to them.

Money is essential for meeting the necessities of life, for keeping good health and earning family respect and security. You know that. Don't spend beyond your means, even for your children.

At your age, it is time you enjoyed life with your spouse and your friends.

Never take for granted that someone will take care of you.

## Chapter 32
### CHUNKING

Our brains will only retain information if it is fed in a certain way. Most of us cannot remember things if we try to soak in too much at one time. Current thinking is that our brains can best handle memorizing things in lists that contain no more than five to nine items.

This doesn't mean you can't remember lists longer than nine items long; it simply means that in order to remember long lists, you should break them down into chunks. Once you've memorized items in short lists, your brain is able to put the chunks together for one big long list.

Local telephone numbers are a good example of chunking. Phone numbers have ten digits. When you use "chunking" to remember, you decrease the number of numbers you are holding in memory by increasing the size of each chunked item. To remember the phone number string 6483191996, try thinking about the string as 648-319-1996 (creating "chunks" of numbers). This breaks the 10 digits into 3 smaller number "chunks." This is particularly helpful when you form chunks that are meaningful or familiar to you (in this case, the last four numbers in the above series are "1996," which can easily be remembered as one chunk of information).

**How to Chunk**

Suppose you needed to purchase the following list of 12 grocery items (and you happen not to have pen and paper handy and you've consciously chosen not to use a peg list):

| | |
|---|---|
| Spring water | Lemonade |
| Sponges | Laundry detergent |
| Apples | Grapes |
| Dishwashing liquid | Milk |
| Coffee | Limes |
| Tangerines | Paper towels |

It would be difficult to remember 12 different items over the 20 minutes or so you need to drive to the supermarket. However, by "chunking" them into 3 subgroups, *fruit, beverages, and household cleaning supplies,* you make the information much more manageable because you've essentially reduced 12 items to three, using each sub-category as a link to its four members. (Remember hypernyms and hyponyms?)

| **Fruit** | **Beverages** | **Cleaning Supplies** |
|---|---|---|
| Apples | Coffee | Dishwashing liquid |
| Tangerines | Milk | Sponges |
| Grapes | Lemonade | Laundry detergent |
| Limes | Spring water | Paper towels |

**Use Chunking to Cram Information**

When you think of all the details you have to remember when you've got important information to absorb, you can easily become overwhelmed. Use chunking to store the information into your short-term memory.

*Here's how:*

Reduce the information into categories. If you can, boil all the information down to five-to-nine big categories.

1. Identify the major categories or concepts. Try to limit the major topics to seven or less.

2. Assign the details to each category and write them down. These details are the main ideas needed to understand the topic or are a part of the whole concept you are concentrating on. (Concepts may be a part of a chapter or chapter titles. Decide which the really important ones are. If there are more than nine major topics, break your work down into another work group. The important point is to give your mind **just enough** work to do.)

3. Then write a short paragraph for each major concept **or** select terms which conform to your major grouping. Identifying your choices gives you the details necessary to objectively check yourself.

4. Start going back and forth from your recall to your notes, reading and testing yourself on your work until

you are comfortable with what you have written. Try reproducing your work, using only the concept titles. Writing the selections down will help.

5. Repeat the steps until you can incorporate all your terms into your concept paragraphs.

By using this method, you are chunking all the important stuff into major concepts that will make you look like a genius!

To review, the way to chunk information:

> Identify important terms; write a definition of each in your own words.
>
> Identify the five-to-seven essential concepts (the chunk). Write about each concept in your own words. Use appropriate terms in each description.
>
> Test yourself on the terms and concepts; repeat until you can do them all.
>
> Write (from memory) your understanding of the concepts and terms. Keep doing it until you can recall the concepts and all the terms with little or no coaching.

---

Music is relaxing and good for your brain, as it improves memory focus and verbal fluency. Music is not only a mood booster, but it maximizes both learning and retention. Listening to music is a mental exercise. It helps keep our mind mentally sharp. Playing an instrument or getting musical training have shown even better results for memory recall. After six months of piano lessons, adults aged 60-85 demonstrated vast improvements in memory, planning skills, speed of information processing, and other cognitive functions.

## Chapter 33
### REPEATING AS A WAY TO MEMORIZE

Repeating is a great memory aid. (But do **not** use repeating to a fault! People might say you're getting old!)

Remember the children's game, "I'm going on a picnic and I'm bringing ...." As each new object is added, the old objects are repeated. People can often remember a large number of objects this way.

When remembering a list of things, you might try a similar concept. Once you are able to remember five items on your list without looking, add a sixth, repeat the whole list from the start, then add a seventh, and so on.

Don't be intimidated by long lists, passages, or equations that you are expected to commit to memory. Break up the information into small bits that you can learn, one step at a time, and you'll be surprised at how easy it can be. You might even utilize chunking techniques, like those discussed earlier, to form meaningful groups that you can learn one at a time

However, in attempting to remember the items in a list, you may easier recall either the **first** two items listed or the **last** two items listed due to the phenomenon of primacy and recency effects.

In the past, when reviewing a list, did you easiest recall the first two or the last two objects? Your answers will help identify your personal style of memory. If you remembered the first two, but not the last two, you may be more **primacy** oriented (and more likely to remember the first items in a list). If you remembered the last two, but not the first, you are probably more **recency** oriented (most likely to remember the last items in a list). ***Primacy effects* and recency effects are terms used in memory research that indicate a person may be more likely to remember the first and/or last things encountered within a list.**

Use these personal strengths to shape and strengthen your memory.

*Here's how:* the next time you have a list to remember, place the most important items in the front or back of the list, depending on your personal strengths. Then, take frequent breaks. During the break, alter the list by moving different words into the primacy or recency positions. Allow enough time during the break for your mind to clear the link with the prior list's occupant of the primacy position.

(There is another, better, way to memorize. It's described in Chapter 46, "Recall Word for Word." Both techniques work.)

---

Malcomb Gladwell has controversially written about the people he thinks make things happen. He identifies three types:

**Connectors** are the people who have a combination of curiosity, self-confidence, sociability, and energy and have a special gift for bringing the world together. Connectors have a truly extraordinary knack for making friends and acquaintances, and are able to span many different worlds as a function of something intrinsic to their personality.

**Mavens** are information specialists, the people we rely upon to connect us with new information. They accumulate knowledge and share it with others. Mavens start "word-of-mouth epidemics" due to their knowledge, social skills, and ability to communicate.

**Salesmen** are persuaders, charismatic people with powerful negotiation skills.

Which are you?

## Chapter 34

### LINK, MEMORY PALACE, or PEG WORDS?

These methods all are memory helpers. What's the difference between them? As a senior, what's best for you?

**Link** depends on a connecting image to lead from one reminder image to the next. If you want to remember the image in the middle, start at the beginning and go forward or start at the end and go backward. There's no way to go to a specific image. For short lists, Link works.

**Memory Palace** is almost the same as Link, except one can go back to a memory location (the dining room, for example) and remember the details. For remembering lists or speeches with many points, Memory Palace is a good technique.

**Peg Words.** Want to know the seventh item in your list? Picture a cow (as you'll soon discover, cow is the peg word for seven) and the connection you made with it. Do the same for the $93^{rd}$ image, a "bum," and connect the image you want to remember with your memory for a bum. You don't have to remember the third number, the fiftieth or the $109^{th}$. You know the place it is in your list (you have a ready-made picture of the number). Just use the number's picture and bring back the connecting image. You've got it!

**As a general rule, peg words are the best for seniors.** A word can be created for any number by associating it with the peg word for that number and the image to be remembered. Add the **non-counting** vowels and w,h,y, and x to the **counting letters** to make words you can easily remember in numerical sequence.

*But, you never know. Examine all three.*

---

My love, you may not be aware of your worth. Many women in the world feel "unworthy." I affirm your strength, beauty, and the importance that you hold as a person ... all qualities that make you the unique woman you are. And when I say "beauty," know that I'm not only referring to your looks, but also to your character. I'm lucky to be a proud friend, husband, lover, and parent with a great woman.

## Chapter 35
## LINK MEMORY and the
## STORY MEMORY METHODS

You can remember any new piece of information by linking it in some ridiculous way to something you already have in your memory! There is no limit to the number of links you can create in this manner.

> **Here is the Link and Story Memory Methods' secret of conscious association:** For the first item to be remembered, create a ridiculous, extraordinary, illogical image in your imagination. Then link it to the next item (which you have already converted into a ridiculous, extra ordinary, illogical image). Go on from there by repeating the process.

**Remembering with the Link Method**

**The Link Method** works by converting the information to be remembered into wild and crazy images and then linking these images together, the first to the second, the second to the third, the third with the fourth, and so on until you have reached the end of your list. Always imagine vivid, totally illogical, humorous pictures of each item or topic. Make it ridiculous and it's a sure connection!

The **Link Method** is probably the most basic memory mnemonic technique. **Linking** is for remembering **things in sequence** like lists, books, speeches, formulas, strings of digits, technical articles, poems, lyrics, and stories. Linked "things" have a high retention level since it is a natural memory method.

The **Story Memory Method** is very similar. It links images together into a story that helps keep events in a logical order. While both techniques are easy to learn, both are slightly unreliable as it is easy to confuse the order of images or forget images in a sequence.

Each method works by creating a graphical image of thoughts to be memorized. There is no limit to the number of links that can be created in this manner. However, creating wild and crazy images representing the information is critically important.

*Here's how:* Do this by following these four steps:

**Substitution** — if the object is abstract or intangible, substitute something that sounds like or reminds you of the item that can be ridiculously pictured in your mind. A ridiculous substitution image is very important. Continue the process by making it

**Out of proportion** — make it larger than life, or expand it by

**Exaggeration**— instead of one, make it "millions," and then give your object

**Action** — make it move.

**There is no word that does not sound like, or make you think of, something in your own language.** Forming substitute words, phrases, or thoughts force you to use your imagination and concentrate. It works! Once you've linked your list together, rehearse it several times. Repetition is the key to remembering.

**Remembering with the Link Method.** Suppose you want to remember this list of counties in the South of England: Avon, Dorset, Somerset, Cornwall, Wiltshire, Devon, Gloucestershire, Hampshire, and Surrey. *Here's how* to link the names, relying on a series of images:

An *Avon* (Avon) lady knocking on a heavy oak *door* (Dorset).

The door opens to show a beautiful **summer** landscape with a *setting sun* (Somerset).

The setting sun shines down onto a field of *corn* (Cornwall).

The corn is so dry it is beginning to *wilt* (Wiltshire).

The wilting stalks slowly droop onto the tail of a sleeping **devil** (Devon).

> The woman impaled a *glossy* (Gloucestershire) **ham** (Hampshire) on the devil's horn when she hit him over the head with it.
>
> Now the devil feels *sorry* (Surrey) he bothered her.

There is no requirement for a plot to tie the sequence of images together. Only images and the links between images are important.

**Remembering with the Story Method**

The **Story Method** is very similar: linking items together with a memorable story using images that are as vivid, strong, and as memorable as possible. The flow of the story and the strength of the images give you the clues for retrieval. While it is quite possible to remember lists of words using the link association only, fitting everything into a story is a better approach. *Here's how:*

> An AVON lady is walking up a path towards a strange house. She is hot and sweating slightly in the heat of *summer* (Somerset). Beside the path someone has planted a giant *corn* in a **wall** (Cornwall), but it's beginning to **wilt** (Wiltshire) in the heat. She knocks on the **door** (Dorset) of the house, which is subsequently opened by the **devil** (Devon).
>
> From the open door, she can see a kitchen in which a servant is smearing honey on a **ham** (Hampshire), making it *glossy* (Gloucestershire) and gleam in bright sunlight streaming in through a window. Panicked by seeing the **devil**, the Avon lady screams *'sorry'* (Surrey), and dashes back down the path.

Which technique (Link or Story) is most valuable? Use the one which best meets your learning objective.

Whatever method chosen, **nothing replaces practice. Practice, practice, practice.**

## Chapter 36
### MEMORY PALACE

The Memory Palace technique is based on the fact that **we're extremely good at remembering places we know.** A "Memory Palace" is a metaphor for any well-known place that you're able to easily visualize and becomes the key to storing and retrieving information.

The Memory Palace concept has been used since ancient Rome and is responsible for some incredible memory feats. It's amazingly effective in all kinds of endeavors which require remembering lots of information in sequence.

Like linking, the Memory Palace technique uses visual associations. The process is simple: take a known image within each location (your **memory** peg), and combine it with the element you want to memorize. **Each memory peg is a distinctive feature of your Memory Palace. The association is unique.**

*Here's how:*

1. **Name your "Palace."** Identify a location and a common path you would take if you walked through the location. I would suggest your house, although any location you know well can be used.

2. **Define the route.** This means always going through the house in the same sequence, usually from left to right, identifying each location (the dining room, for instance). See the distinctive details that stand out as you look around the room, such as paintings, pieces of furniture, and so on. Make sure the locations you choose are distinct from each other so that no location can be mistaken for another. Your route should be one you're very familiar with, a place where you can mentally both see and walk around in with ease. You should be able to recall the details of each room. Every time you use your palace location, it should always proceed along the same specific route.

3. **Memorize the route.** Once you have determined your path and visualized the identifying marks, commit it to

memory. Try visualizing the palace when you are not there, and then check your mental image against each room to make sure you have remembered every location and put them in the correct order. Picture as much detail as possible: make sure your mental image includes the colors, sizes, smells, and any other defining characteristics. Always using this same routine makes the technique much more powerful.

**4. Add what you want to remember to the details of a location.** Do this by mentally associating each piece of information you need to remember with one of the details of each area. Make sure that you place things along your route in the order in which you need to remember them. If you are trying to remember a speech, you might place the first few sentences on your front door, and the next few on the rug you step on as you enter the hall way.

Don't put too much information in any one place. If there are details that must be kept separate from others, put them in different places. For example, if you are trying to remember alphabetically a list of mnemonics, you might remember the first - acronyms - by picturing SCUBA gear on the table in your dining room.

Only place a reminder of what you want to remember. Use something that will jog your memory; use an image that will lead you to your original idea. As you've read many times, make your association crazy, ridiculous, offensive, unusual, extraordinary, animated, nonsensical make a combination that gets remembered!

**5. Review.** Once you have everything in place, go through your palace, room by room. You should be able to remember everything you placed in a room, in the order of the room's details. As you become more confident, you will be able to remember the contents of a specific room on demand.

At this point, you have completed your journey. If you start from the same point and follow the same route, **the memorized items will come to your mind instantly as you look at your home's selected features.** Go from the beginning to the end of your route, paying attention to those features and replaying the scenes in your mind. When you get to the end of your route, turn around and walk in the opposite direction until you get to the starting point. The more relaxed you are, the easier it will be and the more effective your memorization will be.

With just a little experience, the Memory Palace list will stay fresh in your mind for a long time. If you only need to remember the contents of your palace a short time, use your palace again ... and again. However, create a new palace if you want to remember the contents of your palace for a long time.

You can create as many memory palaces as you want, and they can be as simple or as elaborate as you wish. The most important thing is to use locations you are very familiar with. Each palace is a "memory bank," ready to be used to help you memorize anything, anytime.

Associating physical locations with items to be remembered is a powerful memory combination. You can use the same type of technique with just about any visual image that you can divide into specific sections. Here are some places that can be Memory Palaces in the future:

> **Familiar streets in your city.** Your drive/ride to work, or any sequence of streets and physical locations you're familiar with.
>
> **A current or former school.** Imagine the pathway from the classroom to the gym or to the library, or any route imprinted on your mind.
>
> **Place of work.** Imagine the path from your cubicle to the coffee machine or to the rest room.
>
> **Scenery.** Imagine the track you use when jogging in a local park.

The disadvantage of the Memory Palace is that you cannot pick up an entry point other than at the beginning of each entry point (room). This disadvantage is overcome in the Consonant Peg System described in the next chapter.

Following is an example of a Memory Palace path, listing the articles in each room that are memory pegs. It starts in the:

**STUDY**
>File cabinet
>White chair
>Desk
>Fish picture on the wall behind the desk
>Large enclosed cabinet
>Leather chair

**HALL**
>Bench

**BEDROOM with full-sized bed**
>Tray on bed
>Bed
>Chest of drawers
>Round table
>Chair
>Door to closet
>Table against the wall

**ETC.**

Following is an example showing the items used as pegs in the living room of a palace location (based on WikiHow):

**THE LIVING ROOM**
>The living room has six **wrought-iron** bars over each of the windows that face the street. In the room are a brown **chaise lounge,** a **hickory coffee table** lined with **bronze,** and two **Queen Victoria chairs.** A snake with an apple in its mouth is coiled around a leg of

the chaise lounge. On the coffee table is a tea platter which holds a large chunk of **brie** cheese and wheat crackers. A book on the **American Civil War** and a book about the transformation of **ladies' fashion in France** are stacked next to the tea platter. A fireplace crackles in the corner with several **candlesticks** lining the mantle above. Perched between the candlesticks are an ornate little elephant carved out of wood and a poisonous tree frog made of quartz. A large portrait of great-grandfather **Robert E. Traill** hangs above the fireplace. A giant chest, overflowing with gold coins, is tucked between the lounge and the wall.

---

Most heart attacks occur in the day, generally between 6 A.M. and noon. Having a heart attack during the night, when the heart should be most at rest, means that something unusual happened. Sleep apnea may be to blame.

If you take an Aspirin or a baby Aspirin once a day, take it at night. The reason: Aspirin has a 24-hour "half-life;" therefore, if a heart attack happens in the wee hours of the morning, the Aspirin would be strongest in your system.

Aspirin lasts a really long time in the bottle (when it gets old, it smells like vinegar). Crystal Aspirin, a new product, dissolves instantly on the tongue, and works much faster than the tablets.

Keep Aspirin by your bedside.

There are other symptoms of a heart attack besides the pain in the left arm. It could be an intense pain on the chin, nausea, and lots of sweating. Get this: there may be NO pain in the chest during a heart attack.

The majority of people (about 60%) who had a heart attack during their sleep did not wake up. However, if it occurs, and you're lucky, the chest pain may wake you up from your deep sleep. If that happens, immediately dissolve two Aspirins in your mouth and swallow them with a bit of water. Afterwards, call 911. Then phone a neighbor or a family member who lives very close by. Say "heart attack!" Say that you have taken two Aspirins. Take a seat on a chair or sofa near the front door, and wait for help.

**Do Not Lie Down !**

## Chapter 37
## THE CONSONANT and NUMBER PEG SYSTEM

To **really** improve your memory, hang what you want to remember on a peg. Pegs are a great memory system for seniors.

Peg systems are probably the best-known of all the memory techniques. Items to be remembered are "pegged" to certain images in a prearranged order. The system gets its name from words acting as numbered mental "pegs" on which information to be remembered can be attached. Pegs are hooks that locate information in your memory and can be recalled by location. Think of the peg, and the details associated with the peg will pop into your mind.

As you go along, you'll notice there's some repetition of phrases in the reading material.

You need to grasp the peg word concept. A "peg" is just a mental hook on which you hang information. This hook acts as a reminder to help you mentally retrieve whatever is of importance to you. It is a visual mnemonic technique, a fantastic tool. The peg word system converts sequential numbers into consonant sounds, then into words by adding vowels and, finally, to images that can be visualized. The images are visually associated with the word or picture to be remembered.

*Make sense yet?*

The **"Consonant and Number Peg System,"** or "peg words," is ideal for remembering information that must be recalled in any unique order. Peg words improve memory by creating a filing cabinet in your mind. It works by visually associating information you already know with the new facts you want to remember. And it does so to your advantage.

You'll never forget how to count from 1 to 10. However, mentally attaching information you want to remember to numbers is very difficult because both numbers and letters are abstract and hard to visualize. The Peg system solves this problem by making abstract numbers and letters visual. For example:

In the Peg System, the number, "**2**," is represented by the consonant letter "**n**." The process then converts the "n" to a peg word, **"Noah,"** using o, a, and h as fillers from the **non-counting vowels** a, e, i, o, u, and the **non-counting consonants** w, h, y, and x.

Here it is again: The peg words system converts numbers into consonants, then into words by adding vowels and non-counting letters, and, finally, to images. The image is then associated with the word or picture to be remembered. Bizarre images are most easily remembered.

Peg lists can be used over and over.

Before discussing the Consonant and Peg System in detail, some important points:

The system reminds you of what you are supposed to remember. It is a big advantage over rote memorization.

The peg system enables direct retrieval wherever in your list the item is. Other memory systems tie information together effectively, but cannot be used to recall an item directly in its place. With other systems, you must mentally run through the entire link to get to the item you want. With numerical pegs, though, you can immediately say, "Number 4 is the "The William Tell Overture."

To get to the image, you pictured a "rye" bread sandwich (number 4 on the peg word list) with Boston-baked beans poured over the first slice of rye bread, which was being held by an image of Bill Clinton telling a friend about an overture he'd just heard and humming the "Lone Ranger" tune. Another slice of rye bread is on top of Bill's head.

It's an easy image to create in your mind. Try it. It meets the test of being absurd!

You've already read this a couple of times, but it's worth repeating: Pegs can be used over and over. Your brain can distinguish between the same pegs being used multiple times for different information.

If you're comfortable with the concept, take a break and then get ready to become a peg word expert, starting with the next chapter.

***Got it? ... It's great!***

## Chapter 38
### HOW THE PEG WORD SYSTEM WORKS

With the peg word system, you first remember a visual object whose name represents a number. This is the peg word. Then, to memorize items, you visually associate each item of your list with a peg word image. To recall the list, you simply choose the combination of the peg word and the item.

*Here's how:*

Develop a peg list that will enable you to remember anything in any order and be able to recall it in any sequence. Start with establishing consonant sounds for numbers. Familiarize yourself with the consonant sounds. Don't try to memorize anything yet.

| Digit | Consonant Sound |
|---|---|
| 1 | *t or d* |
| 2 | *n* |
| 3 | *m* |
| 4 | *r* |
| 5 | *l* |
| 6 | *sh, ch, soft g, j* |
| 7 | *hard c, k, hard g* |
| 8 | *v, f, ph* |
| 9 | *p or b* |
| 0 | *z, s, soft c* |

Next, make a very visual peg word, using as the first **counting letter** of the word the consonant sound letter (ignore non-counting letters). This sets the place-in-the-list location of your word. No letter is repeated. Here is the list you'll be working with from now on:

| Digit | This Sound | Memory Aid |
|---|---|---|
| 0 | *z, s, soft c* | First sound of the word, zero |
| 1 | *t or d* | The letter t has one down stroke |
| 2 | *n* | The letter n has 2 down strokes |
| 3 | *m* | The letter m has 3 down strokes |

| Digit | This Sound | Memory Aid |
|---|---|---|
| 4 | r | The word 4 ends with an r |
| 5 | l | Roman numeral for 50 is L |
| 6 | sh, ch, soft g, j | The letters **sh** sound almost like "shoe" |
| 7 | k, hard c, hard g | Two sevens can form a lowercase k |
| 8 | v, f | V is ivy (8) climbing a wall |
| 9 | b, p | The number 9 turned around is b |
| 10 | t and s | T and s combine to make 10 |
| a, e, i, o, u, w, h, y, x | | The neutral, non-counting letters |

Here's your challenge for today: Memorize the peg words below which represent the numbers one through 10. Not too hard to do! But, don't go any further until you can say the peg word for any number in or out of order. Then pick out something to remember, associate it with the peg word in a humorous way, wait a few minutes and see if you can recall the image and your item.

Peg words are your tools to remember **anything** by associating the peg and the item together. It's best to join the items in as ridiculous a way as you can imagine. The peg/your word combination forms a sequence that can be recalled in any order, backwards, forward, starting in the middle, or by a specific number. Here's an example:

| Digit | Peg Word | Remember | Visualize |
|---|---|---|---|
| 1 | tie | pillow | A fluffy pillow being worn as a necktie |
| 2 | Noah | Benadryl | Noah carrying a huge bent drill onto the ark |
| 3 | ma | flower | Your mother holding a gigantic flower between her teeth |

| Digit | Peg Word | Remember | Visualize |
|---|---|---|---|
| 4 | rye | car | A huge bottle of rye whiskey being driven down the road |
| 5 | law | fork | A judge holding a gigantic fork instead of a gavel |
| 6 | shoe | computer | You're wearing laptop computers instead of shoes |
| 7 | cow | egg | You're milking a cow and eggs are coming out instead of milk |
| 8 | ivy | pen | Thousands of ball point pens clinging to a wall instead of ivy |
| 9 | bee | scissors | Millions of scissors buzzing around you like bees |
| 10 | toes | DVD | Over-sized DVD's standing between your bare toes |

Don't like the chosen images? Create your own. The goal is to create an environment where the connections you make are most helpful to you. A caveat: don't change the peg words. Change the images as much as you want.

Recall the items by saying one of the numbers. Remember the image you created and the item should come back to you.

Once you've got the 10 peg words down pat, when you want to remember a list, associate a ridiculous image of what you want to remember with a peg word and you've got both the sequence and the item captured.

As you've undoubtedly noticed by now, in the peg lists above, each peg number is associated with one or more consonants. For example, the number 6 is represented by sh, ch, j, and the soft g because the consonants all have similar sounds and the rules for applying the mappings is fixed. A frequently-used peg word for 6 is **"shoe."**

The major advantage of using the phonetic consonant peg words is that the system can easily be expanded using an extension of the first 10 numeric representations. "11" becomes a peg word that uses 2 "t's," and becomes *"tot,"* with the non-counting "o" added. "86" becomes the peg word *fish* (8=f; 6=sh, with the non-counting "i" added).

Consonants, combined with the five non-counting vowels (*a, e, i, o, u,* and the four non-counting letters *w, h, y, x*) become words to specify a location in a list. Take the word representing location and combine with it what it is you want to remember in a way that is outstanding. You've got a lock on position and item. Fantastic! A great example of 100 numbers-to-peg words name conversions, developed by Harry Lorayne, follows this chapter. This is your treasure; don't lose it.

**The peg method is a better memory strategy than other memory systems because it's not dependent on retrieving items in sequence.** In the peg system, you learn a standard set of peg words, each of which denotes its sequence in the list. Then the items you need to remember are linked with the pegs. The peg method can be used to remember in numerical order ideas, concepts, activities, lists, or anything! You can access any item in the list without having to work your way through the whole thing.

With practice, the peg words procedure is a very effective memory technique. The mind, using mnemonic techniques such as peg words, makes mental pictures which result in information better retained than in its original form. The more you use the technique, the faster you will become at associating your peg word and the item you want to remember.

*Say the peg words for one to 10. Do it enough that it's second nature.*

To illustrate the power of names and numbers, on the next page is Lorayne's list of numbers and words, from 1 to 100.

The concept is powerful. It can change your life.

## LORAYNE'S NAMES FOR NUMBERS

| | | | | | | | |
|---|---|---|---|---|---|---|---|
| 1 | tie | 26 | notch | 51 | lot | 76 | cage |
| 2 | noah | 27 | neck | 52 | lion | 77 | coke |
| 3 | ma | 28 | knife | 53 | loom | 78 | cave |
| 4 | rye | 29 | knob | 54 | lure | 79 | cob |
| 5 | law | 30 | mouse | 55 | lily | 80 | fuzz |
| 6 | shoe | 31 | mat | 56 | leech | 81 | fit |
| 7 | cow | 32 | moon | 57 | log | 82 | phone |
| 8 | ivy | 33 | mummy | 58 | lava | 83 | foam |
| 9 | bee | 34 | mower | 59 | lip | 84 | fur |
| 10 | toes | 35 | mule | 60 | cheese | 85 | file |
| 11 | tot | 36 | match | 61 | sheet | 86 | fish |
| 12 | tin | 37 | mug | 62 | chain | 87 | fog |
| 13 | tomb | 38 | movie | 63 | chum | 88 | fife |
| 14 | tire | 39 | mop | 64 | cherry | 89 | bob |
| 15 | towel | 40 | rose | 65 | jail | 90 | bus |
| 16 | dish | 41 | rod | 66 | chochoo | 91 | bat |
| 17 | tack | 42 | rain | 67 | chalk | 92 | bone |
| 18 | dove | 43 | ram | 68 | chef | 93 | bum |
| 19 | tub | 44 | rower | 69 | ship | 94 | bear |
| 20 | nose | 45 | roll | 70 | case | 95 | bell |
| 21 | net | 46 | roach | 71 | cot | 96 | beach |
| 22 | nun | 47 | rock | 72 | coin | 97 | nook |
| 23 | name | 48 | roof | 73 | comb | 98 | puff |
| 24 | Nero | 49 | rope | 74 | car | 99 | pipe |
| 25 | nail | 50 | lace | 75 | coal | 100 | disease |

**Silent letters** are disregarded. For instance, bomb=93, not 939.
**Double letters** are pronounced as one.

*The idea behind peg systems has been traced to the mid-1600s, when it was developed by Henry Herdson. He linked a digit to an object that resembled the number (for example, "1=candle"). Common peg systems in use today include: Number Rhyme, Number Shape, Alphabet Sound Alike, Alphabet Concrete, and the one patterned after Harry Lorayne's work, "Consonant Peg Words." Lorayne's system is the one recommended in this book. The name has been shortened for convenience to "Peg Words."*

## Chapter 39
### YOUR OWN PROOF OF THE PUDDING

OK. Time to go to work. Try out the Consonant Peg Word System. Listed below are digits, peg words, and words to remember. The words could represent anything: your shopping list, the major points in your speech, or any other things you might want to recall in order or at any point in the list. Make as crazy a connection as you can to each Peg Word and Word to Remember. The connection must be joined; the images cannot be side-by-side. For example, you might think of an airplane with ties as wings. Write in the "Your Image" column a reminder of the image you created.

**Create Your Image For The Combination Of Peg Words And List Words**

| Digit | Peg Word | Words To Remember | Your Image |
|---|---|---|---|
| 1 | tie | Airplane | |
| 2 | Noah | Kegs of beer | |
| 3 | ma | Cash register | |
| 4 | rye | Ham | |
| 5 | law | Judge | |
| 6 | shoe | Old lady's home | |
| 7 | cow | Moon | |
| 8 | ivy | University | |
| 9 | bee | Bandages | |
| 10 | toes | Socks | |

If you're uncertain about how to proceed, go back and review the previous chapters. **Practice until you can say the peg word for the numbers one to 10 from memory.** Being able to use the peg words are a major, major point of this book. You can expand the list at your convenience.

---

The principle benefit of being in a relationship is having someone to support you. When single, we often fall prey to loneliness or feel beaten down by life, by people, or events. It is hard to resist these emotions alone. But with a friendly hug and some loving words, we feel so much stronger and able to face up to harsh problems.

## Chapter 40
### REMEMBER NUMBERS, LONG OR SHORT ONES

Knowing how to remember numbers is an important skill since numbers are so much of everyday life. The best way to remember numbers is to **convert numbers to words.** It's a lot easier to remember words than numbers. (It's no trouble to make pictures out of words; it's not so easy with numbers.)

*Here's how:*

1. **Convert the numbers to unchanging peg letters.** Start by finding each number's consonant peg letter equivalent (for example, 4=r; 6=either sh, j, ch, or soft g).

2. Then put the consonant letters together, add needed **non-counting** vowels and letters (a, e, i, o, u, w, h, y, x,) to make a word or a sentence. It's not nearly as complicated as it seems!

For example:

> Take the number **1232**, the number of your post box. *Chunk* the numbers to two sets:
> 12=tin (1=t and 2 =n. Add the non-counting vowel i. The consonants and non-counting vowel combine to "tin").
> 32=man (3=m and 2=n. Add the non-counting vowel a. The result is "man").
> "Tinman" is a picture and a word you'll remember (The Wizard of Oz). You won't forget your post office box number either.

Another example:

> Take the numbers: **9185271952163909211 2**. Convert the numbers to the counting phonetic letters. Here's the result: ***btflnkdblndjmpspnddn***
> *Here's how:*
> (9=p or b. Choose ***b***. 1=t or d. Choose ***t***. 8=f,v,or ph. Choose ***f***. Etc.)

*See how it's done?*

3. Chunk the letters based on how you think the letters will form words (this will require some experimentation). Add non-counting letters and spaces as required to make words. (Here are the **non-counting letters** actually used to make the words: *aeauiuaeoeuuaow.*)

The letters, consisting of a string of counting and non-counting letters, converted to words, becomes **"A Beautiful Naked Blonde Jumps Up and Down."**

I'll bet you'll remember the sentence a lot longer than you'll remember the numbers!

Making this "beautiful" conversion is amazing! But it would take a professional to do it quickly, and even a pro would probably take a little time. Reality for you and me is probably going to be less than 20 digits. Nevertheless, the conversion was pretty impressive.

Another example:

> The Carlsbad Caverns are 1,320 feet deep. See Carlsbad at *demon's* depth. (Counting letters: 1=d; 3=m; 2=n; 0=s. The non-counting letters e and o are added.). The "demon's" association is more easily remembered than abstract numbers would be.

Here is a repeat of the **must know** listing of digits and the letters that are their replacement:

| Digit | Representation |
|---|---|
| 0 | z, s, soft c |
| 1 | t or d |
| 2 | n |
| 3 | m |
| 4 | r |
| 5 | l |
| 6 | sh, j, ch, soft g |
| 7 | k, hard c, hard g |
| 8 | f, v, ph |
| 9 | p or b |
| 10 | t or d and s |

And here are the **non-counting** vowels and letters, a, e, i, o, u, w, h, y, and x, that are available to add to the counting letters to make a word or a sentence.

Think about converting numbers to letters and words. We'll get practical in the next chapter.

> Once the grown-up children have left the house, like a summer breeze, a sudden air of spontaneity enters your life. You delightfully notice it in your love life. Whether you and your partner suddenly decide to embark on a vacation or spend a romantic evening together in bed, you both conclude there are a number of benefits to having an empty nest!

## Chapter 41
### MORE ON NUMBERS

Time to make all this stuff real.

Do you remember the sentence from the previous chapter that stood for a long string of 20 numbers? You know, the one that had a naked blonde doing something? I'll bet you do. Here's the sentence: **"A beautiful naked blonde jumps up and down."** Here are the 20 numbers the sentence represents: "91852719521639092112."

How were the numbers converted into words? **By taking the numbers' consonant sound equivalent, adding non-counting letters and, Bingo, you've got words!** 20 numbers into words was not easy, but once done, you'd have that set of numbers nailed. This conversion skill is something you'll be able to use forever.

How about converting your words back into numbers? **No problem.** *Here's* the sentence with the consonants enlarged: A **b**eau**t**i**ful n**a**k**e**d bl**o**n**d**e **j**u**mps** u**p** a**nd d**o**wn**. Strip out the non-counting letters.

What's the first remaining consonant letter? "b," from beautiful; "b" represents the digit "9." The next consonant is "t." "t;" represents the digit "1." Next is "f," representing "8."

You've got the first 3 three numbers of a 20-digit string, 918. But wait, there's more! Here are all the consonant sounds for the 20 digits: **btflnkdblndjmpspnddn.** *Break it down; "chunk it":* btfl-nkd-blnd-jmps-p-nd-dn. Write below the numbers the consonant sounds represent:

9 1 8 _ - _ _ _ - _ _ _ _ - _ _ _ _ - _ _ _ - _ _ (If you need to, use your peg word chart from the previous chapter.)

Did you come up with "9185 - 971 - 9521 - 6390 - 921 - 12?" Did you ever think you could remember 20 out-of-sequence numbers?

Making words out of numbers is not easy. Harry Lorayne and others have helped us by creating a list of two-digit words representing 1 to a 100. You saw the list at the end of Chapter 38. Use that list to help with the following paragraphs.

Try this: 352364. Chunk the numbers into three groups of two, 35-23-64, then go to Lorayne's list to see what happens. You get this: "mule," "name," "cherry." A mule named Cherry. When you think of the object that the substitution represents, you'll think of a mule named Cherry and remember the numbers you're looking for are 35 – 23 – 64.

See how it works? Pretty neat, huh?

There is an online aid that will help with making words from longer series of numbers. Check http;//www.phoneticmnemonic.com. (Of the many options on-line, it's the least confusing web site.)

***In summary, here's how:***

1. Take your numbers and chunk them into manageable segments.
2. Convert the numbers to consonants.
3. Add vowels and non-counting letters.
4. Make words, or link the words together to make a sentence or story.
5. When you want the numbers back, convert the consonants back to your original numbers.

Sounds easy, doesn't it?
It is.
You can do it.

Note: See Chapter 44, "Forgetting the Routine Stuff is Easy, but Don't," for a way to convert numbers into a story.

---

I know a guy who's addicted to brake fluid, but he says he can stop any time.
I'm reading a book about anti-gravity. I just can't put it down.
I didn't like my beard at first. Then it grew on me.
What do you call a dinosaur with an extensive vocabulary? A thesaurus.
Velcro - what a rip off!
Don't worry about old age; it doesn't last.

## Chapter 42

### Keyword

*"There it was. That word. I know I know it. Think. I know I know it."*

Then your mind begins to do its thing: The sound the word makes is trying to create an image in your mind. After all, your brain is naturally skilled at remembering the unusual. Suddenly, an image pops into your head. It's a huge bear, waving its paws enthusiastically into the air, gesticulating to a group of people sitting in chairs. They're in a courtroom. That's a jury the bear is talking to, trying to make his point. The bear is acting like a lawyer. He's pleading for his client's innocence. That's it! Barrister ... bear ... being a lawyer ... barrister.

**Smile. You got it.**

You've just used the keyword technique. You used the method to help remember that barrister is another word for lawyer. In a previous time you had come across the word, barrister, learned what it meant, and created a keyword, bear, for the unfamiliar word. Now, when you came across the word again, you used a keyword that sounded like barrister, bear; the picture came into your mind and you made the association and understanding.

In actuality, the process requires seconds. And it works!

What you did in that mental exercise met the requirement for creating a keyword trigger. The image actually interacted; it wasn't just a picture of a bear the bear was doing something, it was lawyering.

Keyword triggers can be used to learn new terminology, facts, definitions, language vocabulary, science terms, math formulas, Bible verses, news articles, theories, history, product information, procedures, art and music, computer terms, foreign language vocabulary, dates, figures, theories ... anything. It's an extremely powerful process. The term is not frequently referred to in memory literature, so, if you've been doing research, you may be seeing it here for the first time. "Substitute word" is another name for the technique.

Remember this: A Keyword trigger is the process involving the creation of substitute words and visualization. It's done with the intent to bring a definition to life.

*Here's how:*

First, convert the sound of the keyword you have chosen into images that can be visualized (picture it).

Second, associate those images with an image representing the actual meaning of the word.

**It's natural to remember images easily.** You can imagine all the furniture in the living room of your house without effort, right? It's not hard to call to mind your favorite chair. Certainly, you don't need to "study" the chair or its location in order to remember it. Your brain just does it! You know exactly where the chair is placed in the room. You didn't make a conscious effort to memorize that information. You didn't need to. Here's why:

Your brain is skilled at remembering the unusual. You don't waste memory space on what you ate for breakfast two weeks ago. But when something bizarre, strange, or out of the ordinary happens, you remember it. That's why making an effort to think up weird, even impossible, images is an essential part of the Keyword Method (and of many other memory techniques). Integrating your brain's natural ease of remembering images into the learning process makes it easier to recall information. It does, really.

Then, in addition to creating the image, replace abstract details that are hard to visualize with easy-to-imagine objects or actions that sound like the abstract word.

*That's it!*

The applications of the keyword memorization technique are almost endless. The limit is your imagination.

## Keywords are another application of peg words

The keyword is a "one time" use of the peg word concept. An easily pictured keyword is a trigger word or image that brings to mind the image, word or whatever you're searching for. For example, say you're having a hard time remembering the name of that gorgeous morning-blooming flower in your back yard. It's a Hibiscus. To bring its name to memory anytime, imagine the flower growing very high into the air, with its stem rooted in a very big biscuit. Picture it! A beautiful flower, growing high into the sky with its stem in a very big biscuit. What's its name? High Biscuit, **Hibiscus.**

With this image, you've met the requirement for visualizing an outlandish image that associates with the name you're trying to remember. You've made it an out-of-proportion, bizarre, graphic image that could be joined to an image already stored in your brain. It's a great use of Substitution, Visualization, and Association working together to create a recallable memory.

*What's a barrister?*
After reading the word, I'll bet the first thing that happened was you saw that bear.

**Specialized Vocabulary**
The keyword method can also be used to learn words in a specialized vocabulary. For example, Ranidae is the scientific term for common frogs. A good keyword for Ranidae is rain, along with a picture of frogs hopping in the rain.

It also works with foreign words. In French, s'il vous plait means "please." Think of a silver plate as your keyword. Picture wanting something on a silver plate.

In Portuguese, a woman's purse is a bolsa. The keyword would be a gigantic piece of balsa wood carrying a purse.

**There is no word that does not sound like, or make you think of, something in your own language. Substitution, visualization, and association are the secrets to making images, words, and their definitions easy.**

*Keywords enhance memory. Keyword use is a great way to take in (encode) information so that it will be much easier to remember (retrieve). Relating new information to information already locked in long-term memory creates a memory that will last a very long time.*

**Keyword Techniques**

Here's an example from literature that shows how to memorize a vocabulary keyword using substitute words and association. Keep in mind, the clearer the image, the better the recall.

An "aglet" is the plastic piece at the end of a shoestring. The aglet keeps the shoelace from becoming unraveled. It also helps thread the shoestring through holes when lacing up the shoe.

What's an easy way to remember this strange word? Create a memorable, crazy mental image that reminds you of the sound of the keyword. "Aglet" sounds like "egg lit up." Imagine an "eggman."

See the eggman pulling on the end of your shoelace. As he does this, he lights up. **Aglet.** This picture is strange and impossible, of course. That's what makes it stick in your memory!

Aglet isn't the most useful word to know (unless you're in the shoe business). But it shows that the definition of any word can be remembered by thinking of a bizarre scene that links the meaning of the word to the sound of the syllables in that word.

**Keywords work in any learning environment**

A keyword is a very fast and effective way to link a new fact to an already known, well-learned fact. The main advantage of the keyword method over other strategies for remembering information is that the process is **fast.** Substitute words, visualization, and association are keyword tools!

Keyword strategies can be modified to fit almost any learning environment. The method enhances the recall of complex words or ideas and promotes better retention of material to be learned.

Here's how:
1. **From a conversation, textbook or article, select the most important ideas or facts.** (Effective memorization requires deciding what facts are important enough to remember, the most difficult part of the process.) **Highlight or bold the most important ideas or facts from the passage.**
2. **Summarize the important ideas of the passage. Write a summary sentence that captures the important ideas.**
3. **Create a keyword that provides a mental picture to represent the main idea in the summary sentence (the Keyword reduction).** Add details to the keyword mental picture so it will be easier to remember the main facts.

**Keywords Applied To Complicated And Technical Material**

The keyword trigger strategy can be used to remember a complicated set of facts and technical issues. In the following example from the textbook, the important ideas or facts are bolded:

Three major classes of processes cause the **cycling of carbon** in aquatic and terrestrial systems. The first class includes the *assimilatory and dissimilatory reactions of carbon in photosynthesis and respiration.* The second class includes the *physical exchange of carbon dioxide between the atmosphere and oceans, lakes, and streams.* The third type of process that drives the cycling of carbon consists of *the dissolution and precipitation (deposition) of carbonate compounds as sediments, particularly limestone and dolomite.*

> The keyword summary: Carbon cycles through ecological systems in three ways: (1) photosynthesis and respiration, (2) physical exchange between the atmosphere and bodies of water, and (3) depositing or dissolving mineral sediments such as limestone.

**Working from the summary, Keywords are created that**

create a mental picture that represents the main ideas in the passage (with details added to create a story around the keyword.

*Here's the result:*

> A man on a *sooty bicycle* (the keyword for "carbon cycles") rode into a **greenhouse** ("photosynthesis and respiration"). He put on an air tank and jumped into a pool of *water* ("physical exchange between atmosphere and bodies of water"), where he *chiseled limestone* off the bottom of the pool ("depositing or dissolving mineral sediments such as limestone").
>
> <sub>The example is from "The Savvy Teacher's Guide: Reading Interventions That Work."</sub>

Here's a fun illustration of using a keyword as a trigger. Do you remember the names of Snow White's seven dwarfs? Here's how the keyword technique will help: Think of the seven dwarfs being at the *side* of Snow White. "Side" is your keyword. It reminds you that the names of the dwarfs can be recalled with two "**s**'s," two "**d**'s," and three *"emotions."*

Set this keyword up, picturing at Snow White's *side* two s's, two d's and three emotions.

> Two s's: Snoopy and Sleepy
>
> Two d's: Dopey and Doc
>
> Three emotions: Happy, Grumpy, and Bashful.

In summary, here's how the keyword method works:

> Get the keyword(s) from the source document description.
>
> Develop a vivid and memorable summary as an interactive image from the keyword.
>
> Create a recoverable story.

---

Marriage is a celebration of trust, partnership, tolerance and tenacity. Homer, in the 9th century B.C., observed, "There is nothing more admirable than two people who see eye-to-eye, keeping house as man and wife, confounding their enemies, and delighting their friends."

# Chapter 43
## SOME OTHER WAYS TO REMEMBER

Of course, there are other ways to enhance understanding. Here are some familiar suggestions that will apply to any attempt to improve recall:

**Really Pay Attention**

You'll not remember something that you didn't pay attention to in the first place.

**Promote External Memory**

Many things that need to be remembered would best be written down, a practice known as "external memory."

**Enhance Meaningfulness**

Find ways to relate content to prior knowledge. Draw parallels to real life situations. Develop concrete, meaningful examples so that the content becomes a part of personal experience.

**Use Pictures**

Pictures (photographs or other illustrations) can provide a memory advantage.

**Minimize Interference**

Avoid digressions and emphasize only the critical features of a new topic. Make sure all examples relate directly to the content being covered.

**Promote Active Participation**

If possible, develop keywords that relate to personal experience.

**Promote Active Reasoning**

Actively think through new information, rather than simply repeating it.

### Increase Practice

Information is better remembered if used frequently.

All these strategies assist memory, and all should be considered. However, because the human brain remembers images better than abstract information, images will be more easily and much longer remembered than if you tried to remember by repeating the information to yourself a million times.

**Memorizing requires practice. An important point. Practice. Practice. Practice.**

---

Spend later. Delay spending. It boosts your happiness in two ways: You lengthen your anticipation, which results in a bigger happiness boost. And thinking about your anticipated purchase tends to result in a better decision about how you spend. So you are happier while waiting, and you're happier later as well, because the choice/purchase you eventually make tends to be a smarter one.

## Chapter 44

### FORGETTING THE ROUTINE STUFF IS EASY, BUT DON'T

It's a problem for all of us as we age: we forget the stuff that yesterday could be remembered without a problem. But, for some reason, today it's out of our head! Meetings, addresses, passwords, phone numbers, parking location, historic dates, birthdays, and anniversaries. Where did they go?

What to do? We are constantly being flooded with information. Lately, it seems our aging brains can't handle it. We can't process everything at once. There's too much. We have to make a special effort to remember facts, and that doesn't always work. It seems both insignificant and significant information is gone before you know it.

As you've aged, it seems to be getting worse.

The only way to put information in your long-term memory is to intentionally store it there. **A good way to do this is to add meaning to information.** For example, connect a memory to something you'll never forget, like a holiday: "My cousin Mary's birthday is two weeks after Christmas." That gets you to the general area, but what is the specific date? And what is your last memory of her? What was she doing, where was she doing it? What was the color of her hair? And how old will she be this birthday? Stored away correctly, you can access it later. However, if you don't make a conscious effort to make it a recallable event, it will be gone.

How can a person remember all the information that's only moderately important? After all, you've got lots of stuff to remember that you have to recall every day!

**One way is to construct a short and simple story using the information you want to recall.** For instance, if you need to remember a list of numbers, break them down to a few numbers and give each chunk a part in your story. Say you need to remember the number "921556" as the password to your bank lock box.

Imagine a story in which:

1. Your 92-year-old grandfather, Jack, is in a bank vault with you as your security guard. Jack is wearing a holstered pistol, carrying a long rifle, and wearing a bullet-proof vest. Your grandfather is a retired race car driver.
2. His billed hat shows the logo of the number of his last race car, the "92."
3. Jack has 15 grandchildren.
4. He has spent the last 15 working years as a security guard.
5. He is married to a 56-year-old named Margaret.

When you stand in the bank vault and want to recall the 921556 password, seeing the lockbox image triggers your grandfather's story. Starting with his age, the rest of the numbers will come back to you as you smile and see him in your mind. (To make this story work, your grandfather will always be 92 years old!)

(The Story Method is described in detail in Chapter 35, "Link Memory and the Story Memory Methods.")

---

A man has reached middle age when he has a choice of two temptations and chooses the one that will get him home earlier. However, don't worry about avoiding temptation. As you grow older, it will avoid you. And here's the clincher: you know you're into middle age when you realize that caution is the only thing you care to exercise.

## Chapter 45
### REMEMBER THE CONTENTS OF A BOOK

If you are a serious learner (the emphasis is on *"serious"*), you'll want to remember what you've read in the chapters of a book.

*Here's how:*

Read everything on the book's cover, both outside and inside. If there's a paper cover with a bio of the author, read that. Any endorsements by others? Read them too. The purpose of all this is to give you a little insight into the author, his style, his background, and what others think of him.

Next, read everything before the Table of Contents. Pay attention to the date the book was published and whether you'll be reading the first, second or $99^{th}$ edition. This says a lot about topic currency and sustainability.

Scan the Table of Contents. See how the book is divided up, whether there are obvious changes as the book chapters move towards the last chapter. This tells you things like whether the book covers a transition from the past to the present, is historical or fictional, or whether the book contains lessons applicable today.

Flip through the book looking for anything graphic: pictures, charts, tables, stuff in circles, squares, triangles, rectangles, or boxes, bolded, or capitalized. These things tell your brain to expect something special. Since you and I learn more from pictures than we do from words, graphics begin preparing you for what's next: content.

Begin reading the first chapter. Before you start, ask yourself this question: "What kind of a book did I decide this is?" Is it for fun, for information, historical, or technical reasons ... or ask any question that defines why you're starting out on this journey. Questions prepare you, get you ready to start on a new adventure.

OK. With the first chapter open before you, check to see if the author has summarized the chapter (it will probably be in italics, double-indented); if it is, read it. If the answer was "no," flip over to the last page of the chapter. If there is a summary, read it.

Flip through the chapter and check for sub-heads, descriptive breaks ... anything that indicates the author gave special attention to his following words. Read them.

Start reading from the beginning of the chapter. Don't underline or make any marks on the pages **yet.** Just read. When you've finished a chapter, ask yourself: "What happened? Did I understand?"

Regardless of your answer, now go back and mark on the page margins, underline, highlight, draw arrows, add exclamation marks ... do anything that signals what you **now** think important.

Ask yourself again: "What happened? Did I understand?" (The answer better be "yes," because if it isn't, you're out of your league!)

If what you've read may need to be written answers on a test or included in a speech or a book review, then do this:

For each chapter, write questions on one side of a 3 x 5 card. Write the answer on the other side or a reference to a page in the book. Be sure to ask questions and develop answers to every important topic in the chapter.

When you've finished a chapter, review your questions and answers. If you asked a question that you can't answer, check things out ... again and again ... until you've got answers to every one of your questions.

Now you're ready to start on the next chapter.

How long does this process take? Based on what others have said, too long. You'll probably follow these suggestions only if what you want to learn is life-saving. But this system works.

And so do the other techniques you've read about as you have progressed through this book. You are a memory whiz! You now know what "Kaizen" is. In fact, you've become a devotee (and an expert) of learning in small steps.

> If you give your partner the courage to try things, you have eliminated a wall of negativity. We all have doubts about ourselves, so it is our responsibility to help others overcome their doubts. Do this and you will feel the positivity return straight back to you. Whatever choice your partner has made, it was still their choice. And if you condemn them, they will retreat from you. If you offer them understanding, they will appreciate you and remain close.
>
> You don't have to go bungee-jumping to try something for the first time together. Take a class, start a new hobby, go to a new place, cook together; whatever you can think of. In a way, it is not the activity that matters, but the company you keep. Whatever you fancy doing, invite your partner to join in. Chances are they will say yes.
>
> Sometimes we think that what "I think what I want" and what they want are an either-or situation. Not necessarily so. In business, we negotiate to find a satisfying solution. Relationships work well with the same principle. Tell your partner; "We can do what you want now if we do what I want next time." How could they possibly disagree?

## Chapter 46
### RECALL WORD FOR WORD

At our age, we don't think we'll ever have to repeat some document word-for-word—verbatim. But you never know. This chapter describes an easy way to recall **exactly** the words of an author. Here's the secret:

*Recall, don't repeat.*

Memorizing a document word for word?

It's hard to do. When you memorize by rote (repeating the same thing over and over many, many, many times), you're not using the lessons of this book. Remember exactly by associating or visualizing new material in an unusual way and then linking the new information to other images already in your long term memory.

Recalling, **not** repeating, is the way to store information in our brains. Repeatedly reading something you want to memorize creates different connections in your brain than the act of recalling. **Recalling creates new brain connections. Recalling forces your brain to work for you.**

Believe it or not, it's much easier to memorize by recalling. Repeating is much, much harder.

When you use the recalling technique described in this chapter, it strengthens the same brain pathways that will be activated when you need to remember the information later on. This is good ... and smart.

However, you can't practice recalling the material until the information is at least partially stored in your short term memory.

*Here's how:*

Start by reading the material a couple of times before you start using the recalling technique described in this chapter. The Gettysburg Address is used as the example. Read it a couple of times before proceeding:

Four score and seven years ago, our fathers brought forth on this continent, a new nation, conceived in Liberty, and dedicated to the proposition that all men are created equal.

Now we are engaged in a great civil war, testing whether that nation, or any nation so conceived and so dedicated, can long endure. We are met on a great battlefield of that war. We have come to dedicate a portion of that field as a final resting place for those who here gave their lives that this nation might live. It is altogether fitting and proper that we should do this.

But, in a larger sense, we cannot dedicate — we cannot consecrate — we cannot hallow — this ground. The brave men, living and dead, who struggled here, have consecrated it, far above our poor power to add or detract. The world will little note, nor long remember what we say here, but it can never forget what they did here. It is for us the living, rather, to be dedicated here to the unfinished work which they who fought here have thus far so nobly advanced.

It is rather for us to be here dedicated to the great task remaining before us — that from these honored dead we take increased devotion to that cause for which they gave the last full measure of devotion — that we here highly resolve that these dead shall not have died in vain — that this nation, under God, shall have a new birth of freedom — and that government of the people, by the people, for the people, shall not perish from the earth.

Using this 278-word speech, **the goal is to force your brain to practice recalling the speech–even before it is fully memorized.**

*Scary. Can you do it? Of course.*

Get Lincoln's speech into your mind so your brain has it–even if you can't recall it.

*Here's how:*

1. Read through the speech aloud at least once; several times is better.
2. Copy the text by hand.
3. Read through the text and write a short outline.

4. Have someone else read it to you. The objective is to get a general familiarity with the piece and to give your brain just enough information to recall the original text without re-reading the original.

5. Create a document that shows **just the first letter of each word** of Lincoln's speech. Here is everything stripped out but the first letter of each word of the Gettysburg Address:

F s a s y a o f b f o t c, a n n, c i l, a d t t p t a m a c e.

N w a e i a g c w, t w t n, o a n s c a s d, c l e. W a m o a g b f o t w. W h c t d a p o t f, a a f r p f t w h g t l t t n m l. I i a f a p t w s d t.

B, i a l s, w c n d — w c n c — w c n h — t g. T b m, l a d, w s h, h c i. f a o p p t a o d. T w w l n. n l r w w s h. b i c n f w t d h, I i f u t l, r, t b d h t t u w w t w f h h t f s n a.

I i r f u t b h d t t g t r b u — t f t h d w t i d t t c f w t g t l f m o d — t w h h r t t d s n h d i v — t t n, u G, s h a n b o f — a t g o t p, b t p, f t p, s n p f t e.

6. Now start practicing recalling. Try to repeat the text just by looking at the first letters of each word. You can do it.

As you try to recite the speech while looking only at the letters of the text, you'll probably get part way into it and get confused. Backup a few letters and look beyond the letter you are struggling with to see if you can figure it out. Remember, you're trying to help your brain find the right connections. If you have to, consult the original text, make a note of what confused you and start over.

Once you can do "first letters" you're almost there. Now say the speech without looking at any helps.

If this "first letter" approach is too difficult, try something easier: cover some words, replace some words with blanks, scramble some words, or just show the beginning of each line. All of this will help reinforce the text in your memory until (very soon) you will be able to recall perfectly the whole text.

To maintain what you have learned will only take repeating the material once or twice every other day for a while.

This way of learning is similar to when you first started learning to ride a bicycle—it was much easier when you had someone beside you every time you started to lean to one side or the other. In no time at all you were able to do it on your own.

This technique is much more productive for memorizing verbatim text than anything else. Your goal is to quickly get the words into your short term memory so you can start practicing the recall process that will move the information into long term memory.

**This method works.**

---

A heart attack can be triggered by dehydration. Drinking a glass of water before going to bed avoids a stroke or heart attack.

Why urinate so much at night? Gravity holds water in the lower part of your body when you are upright (legs swell). When you lie down and the lower body seeks to be level with the kidneys, it is then that the kidneys remove the water because it is easier. Water helps flush the toxins out of your body.

Drinking water at a certain time maximizes the water's effectiveness on the body:
2 glasses of water after waking up - helps activate internal organs.
1 glass of water 30 minutes before a meal - helps digestion.
1 glass of water before taking a bath - helps lower blood pressure.
1 glass of water before going to bed - avoids stroke or heart attack.
Water at bed time will also help prevent night time leg cramps. Your leg muscles are seeking hydration when they cramp and wake you up with a Charlie Horse.

## Chapter 47
## REMEMBER NAMES AND FACES

Everyone has a favorite "remember names and faces" system. The one described below is a good one. The technique depends, in the final analysis, on paying attention and association. The key is a person's unique facial features, as you will see.

You run into someone you met a few days ago, but you've already forgotten their name, probably less than 5 minutes after you met them! But you do remember the face! Most of us learn visually instead of orally, which explains why we usually remember faces but are quite bad with names.

You're not alone; remembering names is one of the most common memory problems, especially for seniors. It may be a mental storage is-sue (you didn't pay much attention when you met the person), or your retrieval method didn't work (you can't get the name back when it counts), or it's a combination of both storage and retrieval.

Do you complain about not remembering names and faces because you say you have a bad memory? Actually, you have an untrained memory. We're changing that. To correct this problem, start by becoming more disciplined about how you meet people. You can more easily remember names or faces by using the mnemonic device, FACE, which stands for "Focus, Ask, Comment, and Employ." The FACE technique works. Use it to remember a face and a name.

*Here's how:*

**Focus**–To make sure you'll be able to concentrate on the people you're talking with, clear away any doubts about your appearance. Take the time you need to make sure you look the way you want to look. Comb your hair and straighten your clothing, You may think this is a strange thing to worry about, but if you are thinking about yourself, you will not be able to focus on the other people in the room, and you will certainly forget their names.

Mentally prepare yourself to remember names of new

persons For example, before a meeting or party, review the guest list. Familiarize yourself with the names. As you meet new people, focus on their faces. Imagine they are neighbors, church members, potential clients, new employees or people who can help you advance your important project Focus on their faces. Make eye contact and give them your undivided attention. Everyone is busy and can become distracted.

Zero in on a unique facial feature: eyes, nose, ears, hair, beard, moles, shape of head, double chins, warts, scars ... anything. The added benefit to you is that by concentrating on physical features, the face is being etched into your memory. You want this impression to be what you see when you encounter that person again.

Lock the name and the outstanding feature together. Do it in a way that is so ridiculous you'll never forget the combination. From now on, when you see the physical person in front of you, the name will automatically come up as you connect the features to the name.

Look at them and repeat their name to yourself at least three times. Use it in the conversation, as we tend to remember names used in conversation better than just names. Try giving the name meaning, a substitute name, or rhyme it. For example, if you meet a man named Mark, you can secretly call him, "Mark of the Ark," because he reminds you of Noah. Or you might imagine him marking a paper. The more extra meanings you give to a name, the easier it will be to remember it! (Be sure to spend some time with the names list at the end of this chapter.)

*Ask*– Asking questions about a person's name serves two important purposes:
  It helps to verify the name, and
  It drives the name into your memory.

Ask whether a name is a full name or a nickname or how the person came to have that name. You may want to ask the person how to spell their name. (But be careful, hearing them spell "Smith" might be a little embarrassing!) Then simply repeat the name. You don't want to mispronounce "Joanne" as "Joan." Concentrate on the new person, Joe, in front of you. Say something like, "You and Harold are avid golfers, Joe, What's your handicap these days?"

**Comment**–Make a connection between the name and some-thing with personal meaning to you. For example, if you meet someone named Barbara, you could connect her name with the song, "Barbara Ann," or with Barbara Bush or Barbara Streisand.

Create a mental picture for names that have meaning (like Fox or Carpenter). Develop a standard set of images you can use when a familiar name comes up,For example, picture a blacksmith's hammer for Smith. For names that end in berg, see an iceberg. Of course, there are some names that do not require a substitute word or phrase, like Storm, Bell, Brown, etc.

Some names don't have a meaning but remind you of something tangible (Hudson might remind you of a river). For names that have no meaning, create a substitute word that can be pictured in your mind ("ice cream cone" for Cohen).

Coming up with a substitute doesn't necessarily involve all the sounds in the name, just the main sounds or elements. That main part reminder is enough for your mind to fill in the rest of the name. Making up a substitute for a name forces you to listen, pay attention, and concentrate. *There is absolutely no name you cannot find a substitute word for.*

How do you make an association between the face and the name?

Look at the girl whose name you are trying to remember, the one with the round face, pale skin, glasses, and red hair. Combine her face, complexion, and red hair: she's Irish. St. Patrick is the patron saint of Ireland, so there's an extra clue there when it comes to just looking at her face to recall her name. Looks Irish; Ireland's patron saint is Patrick; Patrick. Her last name is Patrick.

The guy looks like he's been hurrying to get to his destination. Picture him as being in a rush (Rushton) and arriving in the nick of time (thus his first name, Nick).

She has lovely, silver grey hair, so her last name should be easy to remember!

Be careful what you remember about a person. Men can grow or shave off facial hair, and women are more likely to change the style and color of their hair.

Now you've got three of the name-remembering "face" requirements: focusing, creating a substitute name and an identifying facial or physical feature. Here's the fourth:

**Employ** – Use the name in conversation, the final step in remembering. But use the name casually. Don't include it in every sentence; that would be awkward. Try to use the new name once in a conversation, a second time when you introduce the new person to someone else and, finally, when you say goodbye. Do this and you will have employed enough connections to remember the name.

In conclusion, using the face technique leads to this: remember names and faces by depending on the face to tell you the name. When you meet someone, do the drill.

*Here's how:*
Make a **substitute word** for their last name
Identify an **outstanding facial** characteristic
**Link the substitute word and feature** together in an image that is funny, strange, ridiculous, enlarged, etc.

Developing a fabulous memory will not come naturally. Practice, practice, practice. *It's not that hard. You can do it. After all, you're a memory whiz!.*

**When All Else Fails.** Even after you've started using these techniques for remembering people's names, you still may forget a name. What should you do? Never guess. You're better off admitting you have forgotten someone's name than using the wrong name. Try re-introducing yourself, in the hope that it will prompt the other person to do the same. If your spouse is present, ask if they remember the person's name. Or ask them to introduce themselves to the person. You might ask the other person where the two of you last met in the hope that will jog your memory.

As a last resort, confess you've forgotten.

Below are some great examples of ways to make names memorable. Here are some last names and substitute words or phrases developed by *Harry Lorayne*. See how it works?

| | |
|---|---|
| Aarons | air runs |
| Abbott | abbot, I bought |
| Abrams | rams, ape rams |
| Bailey | bale E |
| Baldwin | bald one, bald win |
| Barnett | bar net |
| Callahan | call a hand |
| Cameron | camera on |
| Campbell | soup, camp bell |
| Daley | daily, day |
| Daniels | Dan yells |
| Dawson | door son |

| | |
|---|---|
| Eaton | eat ton, eatin' |
| Egan | he can, again |
| Farber | far bar, far bear |
| Feldman | fell man |
| Fleming | flaming, |
| Garrison | carry son |
| Gerber | go bare, baby food` |
| Gibson | vodka, give son |
| Hamilton | hammer ton |
| Harrison | hairy son |
| Heller | hello |
| Issacs | eye sacks, ice axe |
| Israel | is real, Star of David |
| Jacobs | Jacob's ladder |
| Jerome | chair roam |
| Johnson | Lyndon, yawn son |
| Kaiser | geyser |

---

**Little instead of big.** Studies show that we often get a greater happiness boost out of anticipation than from the actual event itself. So, more and smaller events will give us more frequent anticipation and, consequently, more happiness.

Although we believe "big" things will make us happier, the opposite is actually true. The big event mood boost is often followed by a letdown. The evidence shows smaller things make us happier, over time, than larger, more extraordinary ones. Simply put, a weekly splurge on a fancy coffee will bring more joy to your life than a new car. Really!

## Chapter 48
### WORDS, WHERE DID THEY GO?

**Having trouble remembering ... ahh ... what was it? Oh yes, Words.**

Having a hard time remembering words, names of books, plays, names of actors, old tunes, etc.? This is a universal problem and it gets worse the older we get. It doesn't matter how much we pressure ourselves and try to remember by force, it just won't happen if our mind is preoccupied. But you can remember the missing words.

*Here's how:*

First, let go of stress; it is the killer of memory.

Second, clear your head and focus only on the words you are trying to find. A big problem for memory recall is multiplicity, or concentrating on a few things at once. Sometimes, the word seems to be right on the tip of our tongue, but we can't get to it. Don't worry, it happens all the time and is actually a biological process. Sometimes the pathway in the brain to that word may be blocked. You have to find a way around the blockage.

Third, get those missing words back into your mind. **Do it by not thinking about the word itself, but think of a word that rhymes with it or a word that has similar associations, or that is similar in meaning.**

> For example: You're trying to find the word, "university." It's right on the tip of your tongue, but you can't remember it exactly. When the path to your brain is blocked, no amount of trying to remember will help. Instead, take an alternative route. Remember similar words. Approach the word from a different direction or path. Think of: 'college', 'student', 'place of learning', 'municipality' etc.

Fourth, if the word you're looking for doesn't pop into your head, take a short break. Buy something. Eat something.

Forget your issue for a little while. Your brain will continue working on the project and will suddenly present you with the answer!

---

"Stewardesses" is the longest word typed with only the left hand. "Lollipop" is the longest word typed only with your right hand.

"Dreamt" is the only English word that ends in the letters "mt".

There are only four words in the English language which end in "dous:" tremendous, horrendous, stupendous, and hazardous.

There are two words in the English language that have all five vowels in order: "abstemious" and "facetious."

## Chapter 49
### FORGETTING TO CARRY OUT HUMDRUM TASKS

Did you turn the stove off? Turn on the washing machine? Made sure no lights are left on in the house?

When we do these "always-do-it" tasks, we use a type of long-term memory called "Procedural Memory." It is the chains of action storage area in our brains that holds the things we've learned to do automatically ... like riding a bicycle, tying our shoelaces, or making coffee. Procedural Memory holds the steps to perform routine tasks with no deliberate decisions required (a simple example would be to first check if any lights are on; then, if necessary, to turn them off). These are the chains of memory actions we've learned, but because of the automatic nature of the action, we usually don't concentrate on doing them, we just let our body go through the motions.

There will be times when you think you've forgotten to do one of the Procedural Memory tasks, **but** subsequently discover you did do it. It's no big deal. However, if you find yourself constantly doubting yourself, we can correct that.

*Here's how:*

Attach another action to the action you're obsessing about and use it to make sure you remember doing it. For example, when you turn off the stove, say loudly: "I turned off the stove" to yourself. Or, immediately after you turn off the stove, take a long sip of water.

Any action that will be easy to remember will help. The rule: **when you doubt yourself, it will be much easier to remember your action if you combine it with something else to remember.**

---

Are you officially a "senior?" Retirees don't mind being called "Seniors." The term comes with a 10% discount! Retirees discover that although retirement may be the closing of a chapter of life, it's also a new beginning of a very informal life. Formal attire no longer means "coat and tie;" it means "tied shoes." In fact, there are those of us who believe life begins at retirement. Goodbye tension; hello pension.

## Chapter 50
### A 30-SECOND MEMORY TECHNIQUES SUMMARY

Here's a quick summary of various memory techniques (which won't make sense unless you've read the book):

**Acronym/Reverse Acronym** (Chapters 30, 31): Combine the first letters of words in a list and pronounce as a separate word. It's not an **abbreviation,** which consists of the **pronounced** first letters of the words.

**Acrostic** (Chapter 30)**:** Take the first letter of words in a list and make a sentence that refers to the original words.

**Association** (Many chapters): Remembering is guaranteed if you associate a new memory with an existing one. Interaction between the two is required.

**Book Contents** (Chapter 45): Develop a routine for previewing the contents before reading the book.

**Chunk** (Chapter 32): Break a large grouping into subgroups.

**Keyword** (Chapter 42): Convert the sound of an unfamiliar word to a familiar word (the Keyword) that sounds like some part of the unfamiliar word. When the unfamiliar word is seen or heard, the mind converts the sound to the familiar word and brings to memory the definition or explanation.

**Link** (Chapter 35): Create an in-sequence image (the link) of the to-be-remembered item and associate it to the previous image.

**Lists** (Chapter 39): associate a numerical peg number or word to the "thing" to be remembered.

**Memory Palace** (Chapter 36)**:** Associate easily visualized physical locations with the to-be-remembered things.

**Mnemonics** (Chapters 29, 30): Use list-like characteristics such as steps, stages, parts, or phases (all parts of a structured order), to graphically convert new verbal or written descriptions into images and then associate the new information to information already locked into long-term memory. There are nine generally accepted types of mnemonics.

**Name and Face** (Chapter 47): Associate the "sounds like" name with a prominent physical characteristic. Use the mnemonic device, "FACE" (Focus, Ask, Comment, Employ).

**Numbers** (Chapters 40, 41): Remember numbers by converting each number into a peg consonant. Decide whether the letters can be made into a word or a sentence. Add non-counting vowels and non-counting letters.

**Story** (Chapter 44): Make a group of numbers significant by creating a **story** around each group. Trigger the numbers when seeing the story object.

**Peg** (Chapter 37): An unchanging word location that is an anchor for items to be remembered.

**Peg Number** (Chapter 38): Numbers to be converted to consonants

**Peg Sound** (Chapter 38): A very important consonant sound(s) representing a digit.

**Peg Word** (Chapter 38): A visual object whose name represents a fixed numerical location. Items to be remembered are associated with the visual peg word.

**Peg words** (Chapter 39): Words made from number-identifying consonants and non-counting letters.

**Procedural Memory** (Chapter 49): The "chain of action" things we do automatically.

**Recall word for word** (Chapter 46): Start with the first letter of every word, use the letters as a guide to memorizing. It's better than rote memorization

**Repetition** (Chapter 33): Say the words over and over until they are memorized. Not recommended.

**Routine memories** (Chapter 44): Add unusual content to routine memories that makes the memory stand out.

**Story** (Chapters 35, 44): Make words from numbers and connect them through a story.

**Word(s) (Chapter 48):** Change numbers to words; recall by rhyming, similarity, meaning, conversion back to numbers.

---

THE SIX BEST DOCTORS IN THE WORLD
Sunlight
Rest
Exercise
Diet
Self Confidence, and
Friends
Maintain them and enjoy a healthy life. But do not regret growing old. It is a privilege denied to many.

## Chapter 51
### HELPFUL CONCLUSIONS

Leslie's Law of Memory: you can remember anything if you visually associate it with a known memory or intentionally create a new memory. Always use a helpful technique to aid memorization.

Your memory will always be in one of three states: unconscious, aware, or self-aware. Self-awareness is what you want.

Kaizen Methodology: one small step at a time. It's a great way to learn.

Your memory is your partner ... in everything.

"Peg" memory systems use numbers converted to words as mental pegs on which information to be remembered is attached. This "hook" acts as a reminder to help retrieve pegged information. The system is great for seniors.

"Cognitive dissonance" is the disparity between our thoughts and our action. The tendency is to change our thoughts to match our actions.

"Cognitive bias" is a judgment made as a result of "group think."

All learning is based on substitution, out of proportion images, exaggeration and action. Nothing you are originally aware of can be forgotten (finding it is something else!).

Creative people are polymaths, they have expertise in a number of specific areas.

All memory is based on visualization and association. (This can't be said enough times.)

Accurate recall is an objective memory it can be measured against the original. Subjective memory is not measurable.

Memory is your personal representation of everything outside yourself **and** your unique way to dig it up for later use.

Memories are made by either external or internal motivations. Internal motivation is best.

People are motivated to learn based on their personal "learner" characteristics. There are many learning styles.

Image memory systems work. Use various memory tools for different memory tasks (hammer, saw, screwdriver, etc.).

There are nine types of memory mnemonics (the first letter of the names spell "mnemonics").

Memories are easier made visually. However, you can make verbal memories.

"Chunking" words or numbers into groups makes them easier to remember.

Categorizing information in "like" groups (fruit, menus, etc.) creates the hypernym-hyponym (superior-subordinate) relationship which is easier remembered.

Some people best remember the first words in a list; they are "primary" style learners. Others best remember the last items; they are "recency" style learners. Both work.

---

Senior citizens have taken to texting with gusto. They even have their own vocabulary:
   **BFF:** Best Friend Fainted
   **BYOT:** Bring Your Own Teeth
   **CBM:** Covered by Medicare
   **FWB:** Friend with Beta-blockers
   **LMDO:** Laughing My Dentures Out
   **GGPBL:** Gotta Go, Pacemaker Battery Low!

## Chapter 52
### MISCELLANEOUS INFORMATION
### THE WORLD MEMORY CHAMPIONSHIP CRITERIA

The World Memory Championship typically begins with a qualifying round of four events. Eight top-scoring competitors from the qualifying round advance to the championship round.

**The Qualifying Round**

1. Names and Faces
2. Speed Numbers
3. Speed Cards
4. Poetry

**Names and Faces**

Competitors have 15 minutes to memorize 117 color photos of different people with a first and second name written below each picture.

Once the memorization period is over, competitors are given 20 minutes for recall. Competitors are given the same photos again but without the names and in a different order to that on the memorization sheet.

A point is awarded for every correctly spelled name, either first or last. No points are awarded for phonetic spellings. No more than two names may be presented for recall per image.

**Speed Numbers**

Competitors have five minutes to memorize a list of computer generated numbers, which are presented in rows of 20 digits with 25 rows per page. Competitors must start with the first digit in the first row and continue with consecutive rows. Skipping rows is not permitted. Once a row is skipped, scoring will stop.

Once the memorization period is over, the competitors have 10 minutes for recall. There are two trials for this event, and the best score is awarded.

Twenty points are awarded for every complete row that is correctly recalled in order. Any completed row of 20 that has any mistake will score 0 points.

Scoring will continue until memorized rows have been completed. Points will be awarded for each correct row. (A mistake in a prior or subsequent row will not stop scoring.)

For the final row completed, scoring is done a bit differently. If the final row is partially complete but all the digits are correct, then the points awarded will equal the number of digits recalled.

**Speed Cards**

The object of speed cards is to commit to memory and recall a single pack of 52 playing cards in the shortest possible time. There are two trials for this event, and the best score is awarded.

Competitors will have five minutes to memorize a freshly shuffled pack of 52 playing cards. For those competitors who expect to memorize the complete pack in less than 5 minutes, a judge with a stopwatch will record the precise moment memorization stopped. The recall will take place once the entire five-minute memorization period is complete.

Once the memorization period is over, competitors will have five minutes for recall. Everybody gets a second stack of cards which is in perfect order (i.e., 1 diamonds, 2 diamonds, 3 diamonds, etc.). The second stack of cards must be put in the same sequence as the just-memorized one. After the recall phase, both stacks will be put beside each other on the table. The judge will compare each card from the memorized stack with each card on the recall stack at the same position. If there is a discrepancy, only the cards to that point will be counted.

The competitor who recalls all 52 cards with the shortest memorization time wins the event. If no one correctly recalls an entire pack, one point per card correctly recalled in sequence will be awarded. The first mistake made ends scoring. The best score from two attempts will count.

**Poetry**

Competitors have 15 minutes to memorize a previously unpublished poem. Once the memorization period is over, the competitors will have 20 minutes for recall. Competitors must recall the poem from the beginning by writing it down exactly as it was written (the title and author also score). Competitors must also make it clear where one line ends and another line starts and indicate where lines were omitted from their recall. A maximum of two consecutive omitted lines is allowed. Points are awarded for correctly recalling:

> Every correctly spelled word
> Every incidence of a capital letter
> Each punctuation mark

Each line has a different number of points available. Zero mistakes in the line scores all the points. One or more mistakes in the line scores 0 points. The last line is scored a bit differently from the rest. A partially completed final line of the answer scores the marks for the portion remembered if the line is correct as far as it goes.

Eight competitors from the Qualifying Round advance to the Championship Round.

**The Championship Round**
1. Spoken Words
2. People
3. Double Deck of Cards

**Spoken Words**

Competitors have 15 minutes to memorize a list of 200 words organized numerically in five columns with 20 words per column (two pages). Recall must start at the first word of column one and remember as many of the words as possible. The word list is comprised of concrete nouns, abstract nouns, and verbs.

Once the memorization period is over, the competitors will be randomly ordered to begin the oral recall of words. Recall will begin with the first word in the first column and continue consecutively. Each competitor will be allowed up to 15 seconds to answer. The first three who either identify an incorrect word or fail to recall a word are eliminated.

People

Five competitors will have 15 minutes to hear and review facts about six different people. The information will include: name, date of birth, where they live, phone number, pet, favorite three hobbies, favorite car and favorite three foods. The information will be presented to the group both orally and in a written format.

Once the retention period is over, the competitors will be randomly selected and ordered to begin the oral recall of information. Each of the five people will be brought back, but in a different order than they first appeared. The announcer will then instruct the competitors to begin with the first piece of information and continue consecutively. Each competitor will be allowed no more than 15 seconds to answer. All pieces of information presented must be correct as well as complete.

Each competitor will be allowed three incorrect or incomplete answers before being eliminated. The first two competitors with three errors each will be eliminated.

**Double Deck of Cards (the final event)**

The remaining three competitors will compete in the final event: five minutes to memorize two decks of 52 playing cards. All competitors will have identical decks of cards, previously arranged in the same exact order. The decks of cards will not be mixed and will have different colored backs to distinguish them. The order of memorization and recall (top to bottom or vice versa) will be determined prior to memorization beginning.

Once the memorization period is over, the competitors will have a two minutes' hiatus prior to beginning recall. Competitors will be randomly ordered before the recall period. Each competitor will be allowed no more than 15 seconds to answer. After the competitor calls the card, the judge will flip the card in the master deck to determine if the competitor is correct. The first two competitors to make a mistake are eliminated. The remaining competitor is crowned the Memory Champion.

**USA Memory Championship Records**
    Names and Faces: Nelson Dellis (2015) 201 points
    Random Words: Sophia Hu (2011) 120 words
    Speed Numbers: Alex Mullen (2016) 483 digits
    Poetry: Katherine He (2016) 335 points
    Speed Cards: Alex Mullen (2016) 52 cards in 18.653 seconds, a World Record

---

Government is like a baby: an alimentary canal with a big appetite at one end and no sense of responsibility at the other.

The nearest thing to eternal life we will ever see on this earth is a government program.

Government's view of the economy could be summed up in a few short phrases: If it moves, tax it. If it keeps moving, regulate it. And if it stops moving, subsidize it.

If we ever forget that we're one nation under GOD, then we will be a nation gone under.

DATES
A g 6 LISTS What's
JOKES COMBINAT
HISTORY X
FACES Y 281- r w 15
Encoded PHONE #
24 SHORT RETRIEVED 11
TERM
Names Places LONG TER
SOUNDS ADDRES
U TIME G
POEMS O a V
4 k m W NUMBERS LETT
T MUSIC
I'M LOST S W q U
AGAIN D RECALL
7 8x9= B FIRST
KISS
i Q $ Z HOW DO I?
36 TEACHERS
OLD MOVIE STAR
SCRIPTURES W T p h
n LOOP
LICENSE # M
# A q 12
WHERE I WHERE WE
PARKED RECOLLECT
THE CAR

www.ingramcontent.com/pod-product-compliance
Lightning Source LLC
Chambersburg PA
CBHW070811100426
42742CB00012B/2324